The
Shoebury
Story

Maureen Orford

Ian Henry Publications

ISBN 0 86025 512 3

The picture on the front cover is of the building of the vestry at St Andrew's Church. 1903.
Coastguard Kew
Mr Dalton: Boy Sheppard: M Simpson
A Johnson: H Topsfield: Boy Topsfield: W Johnson
Mr Brice: Revd G Popham
J Offord: Mr Turner: A Harris: Mr Warner: Mr Offord

Published by
Ian Henry Publications, Ltd.
20 Park Drive, Romford, Essex RM1 4LH
and printed in Ireland by
Colour Books Ltd., Dublin.

PREFACE

I can find no complete history book about Shoeburyness on bookshop shelves, so I hope this will remedy the omission.

In 1930 my grandfather, Harry Alexander Blencowe, started to keep hand-written notes always intending to produce a full history himself. A booklet was printed in 1948, but, of necessity, was very small because of paper shortages after the war.

Donald Glennie acknowledged the use of these notes when writing *Gunner's Town*, the story of the Royal Artillery in Shoeburyness.

It is those same notes, pictures, postcards and cuttings collected by my grandfather, supplemented by my own and other people's memories of growing up in Shoebury that prompted me to compile this book, adding other information I have gleaned since I began delving into Shoebury's past.

It is a social history about the people who were here before us. The primitive folk who crossed the inland waterways in their boats adorned themselves with shells and traded with the foreigners who came to these shores.

Of the Roman invaders, and the Danes, whose dominance here was short, and of those who stayed and settled, raising families; the early Anglo-Saxons, the men who came in to build railways and work the brick fields, and the soldiers who served here in the garrison and never left.

I hope this book will evoke many memories for some, and enlighten newcomers to Shoebury who know little of its past.

1999 marked the 150th anniversary of the arrival in Shoebury of the first party of men who laid down the very beginnings of the military presence that was to shape the future of the town for generations to come, but it was not a year for much celebration. The Horseshore Barracks and much of the Old Ranges lay deserted and derelict, awaiting a new owner for a new lease of life.

I hope this book will evoke memories for some and enlighten newcomers to Shoebury who know little of its past.

MAUREEN ORFORD

SHOEBURYNESS

From the Anglo-Saxon *Scoebyrig* meaning fort at the shoe shaped land.

AD 30	Essoberia(m)	Roman
AD 530	Scoebyrig	Saxon
AD 532	Scabirig	
AD 670	Scobrib	
AD 894	Scoebyrig	
AD 1016	Scabrib	
AD 1079	Shobrie	
AD 1210	William De Shobrie held a Knight's Fee in the Honour of Rayleigh in the reign of Henry III.	
AD 1280	Shobyre	
AD 1294	Scewbury	
AD 1412	Screwbury	
AD 1517	Shobery	
AD 1548	Shobury	
AD 1578	Showberye	
AD 1579	South Shoberge	
AD 1584	Shoobery	
AD 1605	Great Shoebury (South Shoebury)	
	Little Shoebury (North Shoebury)	
AD 1620	John Camden refers to the Ness as 'Black Tayle Point'	
AD 1849	Shoeburyness	

From William Camden's *Britannia*, 1695, engraved by Robert Morden

2

FOREWORD

Today there is little evidence that Shoebury was once two very small villages, North Shoebury and South Shoebury, just two of the parishes making up the Rochford Hundred. Time has merged the two together as it has merged Shoebury to its nearest neighbour, Thorpe Bay, and now little remains of their original identity, swallowed up like many other local parishes into the Borough of Southend-on-Sea.

The 'Hundred' was a Saxon term introduced by King Alfred for the sub-division of counties. Each 'hundred' had its own court and appointed one hundred men charged to keep the peace in his own area. The Rochford Hundred, 18 miles across and nine in depth, is bordered on three sides by water; to the north by the River Crouch, to the east by the North Sea, and to the south by the River Thames.

The Parishes of the Rochford Hundred

Ashingdon	Great Stambridge	Little Wakering	Rochford
Barling	Hadleigh	North Shoebury	Shopland
Canewdon	Hawkwell	Paglesham	South Fambridge
Eastwood	Hockley	Prittlewell	South Shoebury
Foulness	Leigh	Rawreth	Southchurch
Great Wakering	Little Stambridge	Rayleigh	Sutton

South Benfleet and Thundersley, previously in the Barnstable Hundred, are now considered part of Rochford Hundred, since they were joined with Rochford under the Poor Law Union in 1834.

In early times much of the land locally was in the hands of a few large landowners: the Crown, religious bodies, or titled families. In mediæval times it was the Barons of Rayleigh, in Tudor times the Earls of Warwick, who lived at Rochford Hall.

As they shared common masters, so these neighbouring parishes shared much of the same early history, and where conditions and descriptions would apply to life in Shoebury I have used stories and examples from other parishes as illustration.

There are few very early records to refer to but there is archæological evidence to support Prehistoric, Bronze Age, Iron Age and Roman occupation locally.

This book charts their early connections, the beginning of a settled community in the Middle Ages, and the rapid expansion that took place in the mid-19th century when the War Office bought land locally. It was this purchase, in 1849, of the promontory known as the 'ness' which is formed by the north bank of the River Thames as it meets the North Sea, that led to it being incorporated into the name of the town.

The geographical location, with part of the coastline facing the river and part facing the sea, made it the ideal position to guard the entrance to the Thames from potential invaders. However, neither the fortified town of the Romans or the Danes were classified as 'forts', the surrounding marshy terrain making it unsuitable for fighting in the event of confrontation with an enemy. In 1539 when Henry VIII drew up his coastal defence plans it was at Tilbury, where the river narrows to half a mile, that fortifications with artillery were built to protect the dockyards further up-river at Deptford and Woolwich, and the river ferry that provided a vital link with Kent.

Shoebury's military associations are with the testing of artillery, the flat open area of the Maplin Sands providing ideal conditions for a firing range as well as facilitating easy retrieval of the shells for examination and possible reuse.

THE RIVER 'SHOE'

This waterway is seldom indicated on modern maps, but earlier maps show it quite clearly. It is most evident today as it meanders through Gunners Park, crossed by light wooden pedestrian bridges, before it enters the concreted gully by the beach.

It is thought to originate from a spring by St Mary's Church and at one time ran directly southward from there into the sea. Its course ran alongside Ness Road, passing behind the camping showroom before crossing under Campfield Road by the telephone exchange and entering Gunners Park.

Stories of the waterway once being used to bring goods inland by barge seem unlikely although this story is still related by older residents.

It would certainly have influenced the position of early settlements as an invaluable source of fresh water.

The north/southward course also provided a natural defensive ditch for the earliest settlers on their western approaches, they were in fact almost encircled by waterways with the creeks extending inland from around Foulness to the north. The whole area was interlaced with waterways providing a means of easy access to inland sites by boat from the coast. Many of these have been filled over the years or just silted up, producing a rich, productive soil ideal for cultivation. The fishing lake in Shoebury Park, Elm Road, is thought to be part of the same waterway, and evidence of reed beds were found on what is now the Friars Estate when the area was being surveyed prior to being built on in the 'eighties supports this.

The Camp. 1905

4

Chapter 1
ROMANS, VIKINGS AND ANCIENT BRITONS

The land that stretches south from the river Roach to the north bank of the river Thames is known as the Barling Terrace, layers of gravel and sand covered by a layer of yellow-brown silt deposited during the ice age. This blanket of sediment, known as brickearth, has provided material for the local brick making industry for many years.

From these gravel layers a rich assortment of artifacts has been uncovered over the years. Preserved by the calcareous nature of the land, they have provided us with clues to the earliest occupants who lived here.

Excavations have revealed evidence of settlements and farming in Shoebury and the surrounding villages dating back to prehistoric times. Some of the excavations were routine workings in the brickfields, or farming, some were specific archæological explorations; the last major of these being 1971-81, prior to the new housing development at North Shoebury around the Asda superstore. More recently, during 1998, an archæological investigation took place within the 78 hectares of Ministry of Defence land prior to its sale. This covered the now-closed Horseshoe Barracks, the site marked on maps as the Danish encampment, and Gunners Park.

In the earliest times this area was one large expanse of untamed forest, water and coastal marshland. Then there were no man-made boundaries to define parishes or named settlements.

During the Stone Age period, before 1800 BC, the people here were wanderers living in small groups, hunting, fishing and gathering fruits and berries. Many bones and fossil shells have been unearthed locally, including a shell necklace worn by one of our prehistoric ancestors, along with many stone and flint implements.

Flints from the Mesolithic and Neolithic periods were found during excavations in Gunners Park, indicating a pattern similar to that already discovered in the Lincoln-shire fens where activity in this period often seemed to centre round river mouths.

Cremation and burial remains of humans and animals have been discovered dating from prehistoric to Saxon times and, at Great Wakering, a section of limb weighing 26 pounds from a prehistoric animal was excavated earlier this century.

Towards the end of this period the people drifting to these shores from the continent brought with them cattle, sheep and grain seeds. They were the first farmers who now began to settle in small social groups, making their own pottery and weaving cloth.

After 1800BC other newcomers known as 'beaker people', because of their characteristic pottery drinking vessels, arrived from the Rhine and Baltic areas. Several shards of this beaker pottery have been found locally. Still later arrivals

Clearly visible from the air, crop marks to the north-west of Shoebury, bordering Eastern Avenue, indicating the site of a Later Bronze Age settlement. Note the double enclosure walls (A), entrance (B) and the site of a roundhouse (C). The other irregular lines, known as ice wedge polygons, were created during the ice age when cracks that opened up in the ground were made even larger by the expanding ice that filled them. The more fertile soil that in time replaced the melted ice produces a distinct pattern in the crops produced today from the continent brought with them bronze tools and weapons, introducing them into the pattern of daily life.

During the Bronze and the following Iron Age frequent flooding was common along this stretch of coast. Large areas appear to have been completely submerged for about 2,000 years by the rising sea, only becoming workable once more during Roman times when the waters receded. The layers of sediment that built up during this time obliterated all evidence of the earlier Stone Age habitations.

This was particularly apparent in Gunners Park, and also to the south west of Bournes Green. Here a large lagoon opened inland from the coast providing a valuable source of extra food. Large piles of shells excavated showed that oysters, cockles, mussels and periwinkles were eaten. Settlers coming here from the Swiss lakes built houses over the water on stilts, accessed by walkways (piers) from the shore, as they had in their homeland. Two large hoards of bronze articles have been unearthed in Shoebury; it is thought they were probably buried by their owners for safekeeping. One hoard found near Richmond Avenue School in 1930 contained bronze articles typical of those of the lake dwellers from Switzerland.

During the following Iron Age people became much more organised socially: they lived in primitive huts and a system of trade evolved across England and with the continent. Metalwork became more refined, gold was used and they decorated and enamelled their belongings with artistic designs.

A defended Iron Age settlement site was uncovered during the MoD survey in the area known as the 'Danish encampment'. It had consisted of four roundhouses, their size indicated by the gullies formed by rainwater dripping from the eaves. Ditches appear to have been used to divide properties or to subdivide different areas of the settlement, as well as for irrigation, drainage and defence. Within a double ditched enclosure a large amount of pottery and ceramic debris was found. Along with high status jars and bowls, there were coarser cooking jars and organic-tempered cooking pots, some known by their type and design to originate from areas across central southern England, Wessex and Somerset.

Whether there was once a house or just a storage facility within the enclosure is not known, but it was clearly a prosperous community, possibly occupied for two or three hundred years, until the arrival of the Romans in this area. Also found were two centrally perforated stones thought to be spindle wheels and a loom weight of fired clay which indicate that spinning and weaving were done there.

There was also evidence of salt manufacture and large amounts of food processing waste. From other sites across Shoebury finds from the Bronze and Iron Age include urns and pots, hearthstones and querns (millstones used for grinding).

Many artifacts found were presented to the museums of Colchester and West Ham, the British Museum and, locally, Priory Park. They include a small mortar and pestle probably used for mixing face paint; a rare penannular amulet with an unusual diagonal hatched design; two bronze keys, a copper bracelet and a ring.

Parts of a chariot wheel were also discovered, with three bronze nails thought to have secured the tyre in place.

North Shoebury, where the land was richer and more fertile with a loamy soil, was much favoured for arable farming. This is supported by the discovery of three differing types of field systems, one from the Bronze Age, another from the later Iron Age which remained in use until the early Saxons, and from early mediæval times rectilinear field boundaries. Postholes, pits, ditches and gullies from the same periods have been found across all of Shoebury, their original purpose not always apparent. Many were used by later generations as refuse tips and middens, the diet of seafood still clearly a favourite, from the piles of discarded shells.

Over the centuries the level of the North Sea has slowly risen and all along the Essex coast discoveries have been made of much earlier occupations that once existed out beyond our current coastline on what was then dry land.

There had been a Roman presence in Britain with trading links established between Essex and Europe long before the invasion and conquest ordered by the Emperor Claudius in AD43. It is thought that Shoebury, known as Essobiriam, was already a fortified outpost as early as AD30, probably as an intermediate staging post between the Roman settlements at Richborough in Kent and Colchester.

The site of that original encampment now lies beneath the mud, the outer ramparts having been built as far out as the main deep water channel. It is thought that the causeway from Wakering Stairs to Foulness Island, known as the Broomway, may have been built as a service road for these Roman settlements.

It is said that in AD31 this community was completely submerged by a tidal wave, a common occurrence shared by many towns along the eastern coast. Those who survived managed to reach the higher land where Rampart Street is today. This street is supposedly built on the original track used by the Romans to travel to and from their now submerged ramparts fronting Dane Street.

One unconfirmed story reports that in AD50 a battle ensued between the local Britons and Romans on the present site of the Officers' Mess in the garrison, in which the Britons, under their leader Caractacus, were defeated. Evidence recently uncovered strongly supports the existence of a Romano-British structure once standing on that site; it appears to have been half-timbered with wattle and daub walls and a tiled roof.

Seven years earlier (43) Caractacus had escaped after his men confronted the invading Roman army when it crossed the river further upstream. His brother, Togodumnus, was killed in the battle. Emperor Claudius had summoned assistance from Rome to quell unrest after the death of their father, King Cunobelinus (immortalised as *Cymbeline* by Shakespeare), who had ruled from Colchester. After landing on the south coast the Roman invaders, under their leader Aulus Plautius, marched across Kent before crossing the Thames *en route* to Colchester. Although the invaders brought much trade to the areas they occupied, and in many places worked in perfect harmony with the local population, their presence also imposed many restrictions and irritations.

The people on the north bank of the Thames belonged to the Trinovante tribe of Essex and parts of Suffolk. In AD60 many would have joined forces to assist their northern neighbours, the Iceni, when they revolted against the Romans under the leadership of their Queen, Boudicca. Together they launched ferocious attacks on Colchester, St Albans and London (Camulodunum, Verulamium and Londinium), looting and burning. 70,000 Romans were killed in the attacks. Their victory was to be short lived; on hearing news of the attacks, Suetonius Paulinus, the military governor for the area, returned hurriedly with his army from Wales and intercepted Boudicca's followers killing 80,000 of them in the conflict, losing only 400 of his own men. Queen Boudicca escaped and fled, poisoning herself rather than face capture.

The Romans abandoned Britain in 426, leaving behind many artifacts from their years of occupation. The long list of items found locally includes wine jars, indented beakers, drinking cups, many domestic utensils and decorated pottery, including Samian ware, a glossy red pottery with embossed designs, imported from Gaul. This was so popular that later, when supplies dwindled, the English began to produce their own.

Many coins have been unearthed, among them a gold one of the Emperor Hadrian, and others dating from the times of Gallienus, Claudius II and Caru. From the Shoebury park area coins of Maximian and Constantinus II were discovered.

Three Roman pot kilns were unearthed in the brickfields near Suttons by labourers working there. The first was found in 1861, nearby was a cinerary urn with human ashes and bones. In 1892 one was damaged when road making was in progress; set below ground level the dome shaped top was broken before it was realised it was there. 500 yards to the south of the first find the third kiln was found in 1895, this being almost perfect and containing 'half a cartload of broken pots', but not one whole pot could be re-constructed from the fragments. Records have identified it as being erected by legionaries of the Imperial Governor Constantine of York, some coins found at the scene were dated from 250-300. The three kilns were in a direct line with each other.

The Romans utilised the shallow tidal inlets for salt pans to manufacture salt, the remains of a raking out pit from a saltern were discovered in Gunners Park, and also managed oyster and seafood beds.

Between 300 and 400 marauders from the German coast had often raided these shores, but now, with the departure of the Romans, they began to stay on and form settlements. These pagan tribes were known as Angles, Saxons and Jutes. The local Britons, used to relying on the Roman army for their protection, were able to muster little resistance against them and finally submitted.

The land here was not very hospitable, covered in dark, heavy forests and fringed around the coast with damp, unhealthy marshes. But the forests did provide shelter and materials to build with, wood for fires and, along with the heaths, provided grazing for animals. Their wooden houses were made weatherproof with thatched roofs and walls of wattle and daub.

Hunting supplemented the meat, milk and cheese obtained from domestic animals, which also provided wool and hides for clothing and bedding. The bone and horn were used for implements and adornment.

The Saxon word Scoebyrig, 'fort at the shoe shaped land', is the origin of the name Shoebury, 'naess' meant headland. All the villages in the Rochford Hundred were given descriptive names by these early settlers to identify them.

Assandun	'Assas' hill	Paeccelsham	'Paeccels' hamlet
Baerlingum	people of Baerla	Raeccesford	ford of the hunting dog
Caningadun	hill of Canas' people	Raegeleah	wild she goat clearing
Eastwudu	east wood	Scopingland	land with the sheds
Hacawielle	hooked stream	Stanbrycg	stone bridge
Haedleah	heath clearing	Sudcirice	south church
Hoccasleah	'Hoccas' clearing	Sud Fennbrycg	bridge over the fen
Leah	clearing	Suoton	south farm
Pritolwielle	babbling brook	Waeceringas	settlement of Waecer

At North Shoebury a Saxon burial ground was discovered, the bodies had been placed in a circle like the spokes of a wheel, with feet innermost. Similar graves have been found in Buckinghamshire and Vendhuile, in France. Also found were the remains of a small Saxon cremation site. These Saxons worshipped in groves of trees.

A small needlework set with a tiny pair of shears and an early dolphin buckle found locally date from this period, as does a lead token thought to have been used in trade.

Nearly 500 years after the Romans suffered from a watery fate, so too did these East Saxon settlers as once again the sea inundated the area.

From 793 the Vikings came to plunder Europe's shores. Shoebury, for a short time, became the base for a group that fled here after the Battle of Benfleet in 894. However, they did not stay and settle like the Saxons. It had begun two years earlier when two groups of Danish invaders crossed from Boulogne in France to Kent. The largest company (whose leader is unrecorded) came in 250 ships which landed in the River Lymphe and camped at Appledore. A second, smaller contingent led by Haesten, arrived in 80 ships and landed at Milton, in a small creek off the main channel between the island of Sheppey and the mainland.

The arrivals met with little opposition, but, wanting to keep the two armies apart, Saxon King Alfred positioned his men between them. He arranged a peaceful treaty with Haesten, who left Kent with his men for Essex. The larger company, however, set off on raiding forays as far away as Hampshire and Berkshire. When they turned, planning to unite once more with Haesten's group, they were intercepted by the West Saxon militia under Alfred's eldest son, Edward, at Farnham. In the ensuing battle they were defeated and the Danish king badly injured, so they hastily retreated to an island in the River Colne, near Iver.

Without the assistance of his father's army, which was in Exeter, Edward felt his army was not strong enough to risk another attack so a stalemate was agreed. Under this the Danes were to depart peacefully from England, but instead they regrouped with their allies further east at Benfleet, forming a much larger force under Haesten.

When this larger group left to go raiding in Mercia an army of men from the East Wessex militia and the Garrison of London, assisted by reinforcements from the west, attacked the camp. They captured the Danish ships and all the looted goods and took the women and children, including Haesten's wife and two sons. Later they were released as a matter of honour as King Alfred was godfather to the children. Many of the ships were taken to Rochester or London, others were broken and burned. Charred remains of these boats were unearthed during excavation works for the construction of Benfleet railway station in 1853-4.

When Haesten returned, the combined force hastily retreated to Scoebyrig, where they were joined by reinforcements from East Anglia and Northumbria. They proceeded to build an outer line of defensive ditches or pits to protect themselves should they be pursued. Adjoining trees provided extra cover to hide in and sentries used the tops of the trees as observation posts to watch for any enemy approach. Pits were found at Thorpe Bay and Southchurch, and further inland at Wakering and Barling. This enabled them to vacate the first line of defence and retreat in a northerly direction if danger threatened, the vacated pits were then flooded with water from a spring that came from the direction of Rochford.

Until recently it has always been accepted that it was the Danes who built the fortified rampart that lies within the garrison boundary, the northern edge of which followed a similar line to the earlier Roman path along Rampart Street. However, excavation of the site during the summer of '98 revealed little evidence of Danish origin, but items dating from the earlier Iron Age period. It seems likely that the Danes merely used an existing, defensive earthwork from that period for their relatively short stay here.

The rampart was a built in a crescent shape open to the sea, which afforded protection for any boats that were drawn up into the shelter of the crescent, a palisade would then have closed off the opening for protection. The massive bank, a formidable 12 feet high, curved around extending 700 feet inland and measuring 1,600 feet across at the seaward side, possibly even larger when first built before time eroded it. This banked wall was flanked by a protective trench on the outside measuring 40 feet across and deeper than the height of a man. Although now a protected monument, only a small section of the rampart, resembling little more than a shallow slope, remains today.

Realising there was little potential here to make good their losses, Haesten and his forces left to pursue their interests on raids along the Thames Valley. It is said they were eventually forced to eat their own horses to avoid starvation. A coin was found locally dating from Alfred's reign.

King Sweyn of Denmark and his son, Canute, sailed to England with a large force in 1013 intent on taking over the country in revenge for the death of the king's sister, Gunhilda, who had been killed in a massacre ordered by King Ethelred II (the Unready) in an attempt to rid himself of the troublesome Danes. Attempts to buy them off with payments of money (Danegeld) only encouraged more to arrive.

Sweyn had made several earlier forays to these shores for plunder and was feared greatly. On hearing of his impending approach the monks from Prittlewell prepared a camp and boats on the marshes at Shoebury in readiness should they need to flee. This camp later became the site of Suttons. Sweyn succeeded in his attempt and became the King of England, but died early in 1014 from natural causes. Ethelred, who had fled to Normandy in fear of Sweyn's impending arrival, was recalled to rule.

His son and successor, Edmund Ironside, then faced a challenge for the throne from Sweyn's son, Canute (or Cnut). These two young Kings fought a total of six pitched battles, the last being at Assandun (Ashingdon) when the English confronted Canute and his men, who were retreating from Canewdon to rejoin their ships at Sheppey.

After a long, hard battle the English forces were pushed back over the River Crouch and defeated at Battlesbridge on St Luke's Day, 18th October, 1016. The triumphant Danes marched back to the encampments at Scabrib (Shoebury) to celebrate.

Out of a mutual respect for each other the two contenders for the throne then divided the rule of the land between themselves, but Edmund died within a year of finally becoming king and the whole realm then came under Canute's rule.

While he resided at Canewdon, between 1020 and 1024, King Canute often came to the sands at Scabrib to shoot wild fowl. A coin from this period was discovered locally.

Chapter Two
FROM DOMESDAY TO THE REFORMATION

Life changed dramatically after William of Normandy took the English throne in 1066. The lands of those who had supported Harold were confiscated and divided into portions, called knight's fees, and distributed amongst William's henchmen. Each received enough land to support himself and his followers, and in return ensured a ready force of armed men to be called upon by the King in an emergency or war. The 'fees' were not apportioned equally so some 'barons', as the these Normans were called, who had received very large fees sublet parts of their estates which allowed many of the Saxon thanes to remain on their lands as tenants.

Unlike other parts of the country which experienced great changes after the conquest as land changed hands, the local area suffered relatively little upheaval as much of the land in Shoebury and the surrounding parishes remained under the ownership of Robert Fitz-Wimarc of Clavering, Baron of Rayleigh.

He was the only pre-Norman landowner to retain all his lands after the Conquest in 1066, therefore things continued much as they had done before. He must certainly have been well trusted to have been allowed to hold such a large expanse of land in one area, in total 9,000 acres; usually land awards were spaced well apart to stop too much control by one person in an area. In the Rochford Hundred he had 130 tenants and 50 knights under him. 4,000 sheep grazed on the marshland fringes of the estates.

Robert was the Sheriff of Essex, Chancellor, and hereditary Standard Bearer to the Crown during both Edward the Confessor's (1042-1066), and William the Conqueror's reigns, being the close confidant of both. It is thought he was of Danish origin related to William's mother, which might explain how he managed to retain his lands.

Elsewhere landowners who had not fought at Hastings were allowed to 'buy back their lands'. They paid a fine, made a formal surrender of their properties and received them back under the new feudal obligations, now becoming tenants-in-chief, no longer freeholders but personal dependants and vassals of the crown.

Between 1080 and 1086, William ordered a survey of all the lands in his kingdom, with only a few counties not included. This census was to determine the name of every landowner, the valuation of his estate, and how it was made up, *i.e.* wood, meadow, arable, or pasture, and an account of the service and money due from him to the King. The 'Domesday Book' served also as a population count, dividing people by status and also drew comparison between the current facts and those 20 years earlier at the time of King Edward.

The record for South Shoebury:

Essoberiam was held by Robert the son of Wimarc after the death of King Edward: now by Suene by demesne for 1 Manor and for 5 hides.

Always 9 Villeins [tenants].   Then 4 bordars [servants] ...... now 6.

Always 2 teams [ploughs] in the demesne [manor], and 8 teams of the homagers [the men]: 3 acres of meadow. Wood for 20 swine.

Then 2 horses, 4 beasts,   12 swine, 100. sheep:

Now 2 horses,   -----   16 swine 64 sheep.

Then and afterwards it was worth 6 pounds ... now £10

8 oxen= 1 plough.

The record for North Shoebury records:

In Edward the Confessor's time it was held by an unknown Freeman for 1 manor and 4 hides.

At the time of the survey Suene held it, with his undertenant, Walter, at the Hall.

Always 4 villeins. Then 6 bordars... now 8. Then 2 serfs [farmworkers].

Always 1 horse. Then 2 beasts, 40 sheep.

Now 6 beasts, 1 swine, 115 sheep.

Woodland for 12 swine (A freeman held the 4th hide [100-120 acres] with pasture for 100 sheep) Then worth £6... now £8.

It is recorded that Odo, Bishop of Bayeux, half-brother to the Conqueror, held the nearby manor of Soberia: it was held by 1 freeman for 1 hide and 30 acres, pasture for 40 sheep, and was formerly worth 40 shillings, now 55.

Sometimes North Shoebury was known as Little Shoebury to distinguish it from Great (South) Shoebury.

In 1107 the lands of Robert Fitz Wimarc were inherited by his son Suene, who, on becoming the Baron of Rayleigh, built Rayleigh Castle. On his death his son, Robert de Essex (Fitz-Suene), inherited his estates. Next they passed to his son, Henry de Essex, who was the Constable of Essex.

In 1163 he was called upon by Henry II to fight with him against the Welsh at the Battle of Coleshull in Wales. He was charged with cowardice when, acting as standard bearer, he fled the battlefield. This action caused confusion among the King's followers who assumed that he must have been killed, and in the uncertainty that followed the Welsh took the advantage and beat the army. His desertion was deemed to be high treason and he was obliged, as was the custom, to fight for his freedom in single combat. His duel, which he lost, was fought with Robert de Montfort, but he was spared the customary death penalty and banished, as a monk, to the abbey at Reading. His estates were forfeited to the Crown, a welcome addition to King Henry's exchequer.

The new Norman masters were not always benevolent, often very cruel, 'cold heart and bloody hand now rule this English land' the saying went. They had brought a new language, laws and customs to the English people and under them life began to take on a more structured pattern. From these new masters the Saxons gained builders, knights, and scholars and connections with the continent. So began a new mixed race with a mixed dialect - the reason we often have more than one word for the same thing today, one stemming from the Saxon word, the other derived from the Norman French language.

THE FIRST LANDMARKS

In this period many buildings were established that we know today.

Started in the reign of William II, the building of St Andrew's Church was not completed until 1100, when Henry I was on the throne; the square tower of typical Norman design was clearly visible to ships passing in the estuary. South Shoebury was then a small fishing village and the church was named for St Andrew, the fisherman. The church ornamentation and carvings also reflect this connection with the sea.

A little later in North Shoebury St Mary's Church was built over a reed bed.

In 1206 a parsonage was built in a small wooded grove some distance from St Andrew's, linked by a pathway crossing the common land to a stile at the front of the church. Around both churches the surrounding rural countryside supported the small, scattered population. There was no village at this time, only a few isolated homesteads.

In the 12th century Robert de Essex built South Shoebury Hall, bordering the eastern side of St Andrew's Church. He gave this house and a pasture called Muschall Grange to the monks of the Cluniac order, as well as other lands and property, including Prittlewell Manor on the site of which they built Prittlewell Priory. Every year on the feast of St Pancras payment was made from Prittlewell to the mother priory at Lewes, Sussex, of one mark of silver. The order had been founded in Burgundy in 910 as an offshoot of the Benedictines.

It was not uncommon at this time for gifts of land and property to be given to the church. This, the donor hoped, would ensure a favourable reception when the time arrived for him to depart this life and enter God's kingdom. Robert's gifts were made for 'the salvation of my soul and of my wife, and my father, and my mother, and of Beatrice my grandmother and of all those whose care it may be to maintain and increase that place'. For 400 years the monks were the biggest property owners in England until the suppression of the monasteries by Henry VIII in 1536, when their lands were forfeited and sold, or granted by Henry as gifts to the gentry.

It is recorded that John Friend held Shoebury Manor in 1220.

In North Shoebury, the manor previously known as Soberia was renamed the Manor of Kents, after the family of Richard Kent(e), the name appearing in 14th century records. The Fitz-Simon family held it in 1328, and for several generations.

Then it was owned by several generations of a family called Baker. In 1594 in an account of the area by the topographer, John Norden, it was referred to as 'a house of account'.

North Shoebury was divided in the reign of Edward IV (1272-1307), and the house was renamed West Hall. The De Wodenham family from Woodham Ferrers who occupied the Hall from 1265 held the manor house for two centuries. The house was rebuilt in Elizabethan style in the 16th century. Adjacent to the Hall on North Shoebury Hall Farm site, three sides of a mediæval enclosure ditch were discovered.

The White House is first recorded as 'Barbers' from the family of Peter Barber who lived there in the reign of Edward III (1327-77); it passed down in that family for several generations. From them it passed to several generations of the Jugo family, then to William Strangman 'by the service of one-fifteenth of a knight's fee'.

Friends Farm was situated on the marshes near the sea and straddled the boundary of North Shoebury and Great Wakering, it takes its name from John Frend.

In 1419 the family of John Croucheman appears in records with the house of this name in Poynter's Lane, at the 'T' junction with Wakering Road.

Bunter's Well was originally one of the outer pits dug by Haesten's men in the 9th century and provided a constant supply of fresh sparkling water that would overflow to the marshes and into the sea. During the 15th century it was renowned amongst mariners and many others. Owing to the traffic to and from the well and the danger of the well sides collapsing, a man named Bunter was put in sole charge. He alone had the right to draw the water and it was his duty to keep the well in good repair. He built a small, thatched cottage nearby which was shaded by willow and elder trees; people came long distances to refresh themselves at the well and rest under the trees. The cottage was pulled down in 1840 and was commemorated with a stone marker when the new promenade was built in 1908. The new coastguard station was built there in 1881, today it is the site of the car park at Thorpe Bay Yacht Club.

The original Shore House was constructed in 1079 of timber gathered from the wreckage of ships destroyed on the shore. The house was erected to house the foreman in charge of ships' cargoes, which were stored in sheds on ground adjoining the house before being redistributed around the district.

The ships arrived and anchored offshore, often carrying coal, wood and chalk as cargo. Wagons, drawn by horses, were taken alongside the ships when the tide was out and when loaded returned up the right of way to the foreshore where they deposited their loads for storage or direct sale to people at Shore House. As more wreckage came ashore the house gradually increased in size. There was a large staircase facing the sea, which could be completely blocked off by lowering a heavy wooden platform across the top and securing it in place with bolts. Apertures, placed either side at the top, housed firearms, used to deter unwelcome visitors attempting to ascend. A large amount of smuggling was done here from the ships, and wrecking was not uncommon along this whole stretch of the coast. Inquests on bodies found drowned were held at what is now the Halfway House public house.

In 1084, under terms laid down in the Domesday Survey, a new house was built as a resting place for the monks on the marshland at Suttons, on the site of the old camp set up in 1018 for the monks should they need to flee from the Danish King Sweyn. This house was destroyed in 1290 and a new mansion, called Shoebury Hall, was built on the site four years later.

THE WAY OF LIFE

Between 1066-1300 settlement at North Shoebury had centred round a large enclosure south-east of St Mary's church: it was rectangular, surrounded by a ditch four metres wide and 1½ metres deep. After 1300 the settlement moved to cluster nearer West Hall. Here the remains of suckling pigs, animal bones, and grains have been excavated, as well as fragments of imported ceramics and decorated pottery indicating the finer lifestyle compatible with a manor.

As the population was small the area set aside for cultivation was not large. The first subsistence farmers had made forest clearings to plant their few crops, but now the range of produce had become more varied and there was some trade with neighbouring districts. Cereal and root crops were grown. Wheat (in particular at North Shoebury), oats, barley, rye, beans and mustard. A small amount of wheat was also exported, illegally at times when prices on the continent rose sharply and it was a more profitable market. The heavy clay soil was enriched with manure (sewage) brought down from London and chalk from Kent.

This pattern of farming continued with few changes until the mid-16th century when the Reformation saw an end to the manorial system, when the Lord of the Manor and the monasteries no longer owned all the land and reaped all the benefits, the land was once again let to tenant farmers who farmed independently.

There is also evidence of mediæval settlement around the area of the garrison church. The gravelly nature of the soil around South Shoebury and the Ness was less productive, so there the heaths and marshy areas were used mainly for grazing sheep and wild-fowling. The constant advance and retreat of the sea over the centuries had resulted in large areas of salt marsh forming along the coast, made up of alternating layers of muddy silt and peat, stabilised by the plants that grew there. This provided ideal grazing for large flocks of sheep and is referred to in the survey as 'pasture'. Inland manors often included stretches of grazing land on coastal marshland in their possessions. Sheep were the mainstay of the local farmers, providing not only meat and wool and skins for parchment but, during the summer time, milk as well. This would be made into butter and the ewes' milk used to make cheeses.

17

The local marshland wool was coarse and thus fetched a low price. In 1343 each sack fetched 4 marks less than that from other areas of Essex. It would be taken by boat up the Thames to the markets of London, or by sea to Flanders where there was a great weaving trade. By comparison cattle farming was on a much smaller scale as the damp, soggy ground caused foot rot in the animals, but swine, pigs and goats were kept and also bees.

The main method of catching fish was in 'weirs'. Supported by posts these triangular enclosures made of woven twigs were open on the shore side to trap the fish when the tide receded. Similarly constructed triangular 'kiddles' made of netting were also used. The fish were collected at low tide and brought ashore by horse and cart. Long line fishing on the sands was another method - still in use today. Plaice, dabs, sole and flounders were the most predominant catch. At the time of the survey almost fifty salt pans were recorded in the protected tidal inlets around the Essex marshes, shellfish still flourished there.

LAW AND DISORDER

During the 14th century there was widespread discontent amongst the working classes, especially the impoverished agriculture workers.

The large areas of land set aside as Royal Forests was just one their grievances. The Saxon word 'greenwood' had always signified an open space of freedom and liberty to roam, but the new forest laws introduced by the Normans (the forerunner of our game laws) strictly restricted access to them by the introduction of entrance tolls.

In the Rochford Hundred these forests were at Rochford, Rayleigh and Hadleigh. Those not allowed to enter were required, on reaching the age of 21 years, to swear an oath agreeing not or cause damage to the forests or to poach there. The penalty in 1279 for poaching deer, boar or hares in the forests was to lose one's eyesight. Hares were designated as 'honorary deer', thus ensuring they remained a delicacy for the rich, the poor having to be content with rabbit.

There appeared to be one rule for the rich and another for the poor when that year Richard de Southchurch, a noble gentleman of dubious reputation who lived at Southchurch Hall, was merely fined a sum of 100 shillings for killing a deer. Many doubted that it was ever collected. Although being knighted for his services as Sheriff of Essex in 1265-7, this wily gentleman found himself an inmate of Fleet Prison in 1285. It seems much of the property and goods he seized from the public in the name of King Henry III failed to benefit the exchequer as intended, but somehow ended up at Southchurch instead.

Nevertheless, this harsh threat failed to discourage poaching or the collection of wood, probably done out of sheer necessity as the working classes were very poor. Any steps to curb these activities were met with fierce opposition, sometimes violence. In 1314 there was destruction of the fences of the royal forests, in 1338 the courthouse at Rayleigh was burnt down, and in 1352 rioting was reported. The Normans apparent disregard of 'greenwood rights' by the imposition of private forests was, the Saxons felt, justly repaid when, in separate incidents over the years, two sons and a grandson of William the Conqueror died in hunting accidents in Royal Forests elsewhere.

In 1349 the virulent bubonic plague known as the Black Death, which had spread rapidly from Asia across the continents, wiped out almost 40% of the English labour force. The countryside was in disarray, cattle went untended and crops remained unharvested in the fields. Farmers were now desperate for labour.

Feeling more assured of their bargaining power, the workers became less servile and began to look further afield for work. The feudal system that had bound them to one master in the past gradually began to crumble, but bad working conditions, high rents, heavy taxes and low fixed wages still remained, the latter pegged by the government trying to keep them at pre-plague levels by the Statute of Labourers, 1351. Tired of their situation, hostility finally flared openly against the government when new laws were passed in 1380 further increasing taxes to raise finance for the war with France.

Shoebury is known to have sent a contingent of men to support the Peasants' Revolt that finally ensued in 1381. Along with others from all over the country they rallied under Wat Tyler, to demand an end to the harsh system of taxes, serfdom and feudal services that was still causing many of them so much hardship. In June the protesters held London and Richard II reluctantly agreed to meet their demands, after apparent victory many of them returned home. But next day the continuing rally at Smithfield broke up in disarray when Tyler was fatally wounded after shaking hands with the King, who immediately went back on his word.

Local protesters then learned that the tax collector was still demanding outstanding taxes from men at Fobbing and Corringham that they believed had been waived in the agreement. Summoned to appear at Brentwood the men had refused to pay and their supporters had chased the official out of town. Alarmed and fearing reprisals they toured the district to enlist more men to assist them.

The contingent from Shoebury, led by local men, John Syrat and John Hurt, joined the angry crowd who caught and beheaded the tax collectors, clerks and jurors; their heads carried aloft on pikes as the mob marched once more in defiance. In the uprising hundreds of protesters had died at the hands of the King's men, but five hundred local men who begged for pardon were released on payment of fines to their masters and the Crown.

During the French wars there was a constant fear of invasion. In 1305, and again in 1385, the whole district was on standby but the threats did not materialise. In 1385 John Wodeham and John Fitz-Simond, landowners of North Shoebury, were responsible locally to rally a defence force of any local able-bodied men, archers and men-at-arms. They were to assemble at the coast in the event of a possible invasion and, if instructed by the government, warning beacons were to be lit to warn other parishes.

In 1386 accusations were made by Peter Mark, a merchant of Florence, and Gerard Lomelyn, a merchant of Genoa, after their ship had run aground at South Shoebury. They claimed that men of the district had looted twenty-two bales of pepper and other goods when the crew had been forced to take refuge ashore. Sir John Fitz-Simond and John Osborn were appointed to deal with the matter when litigation followed.

In 1419 Edward Wodham of Little Shoebury granted to Nicolas Fitz-Simond all his rights on the lands called Barbours.

Shoebury Cross House and the shop at the 'three wont way'

The Pyghtle in use as farm cottages for workers at Danger Farm

Chapter 3
AFTER THE REFORMATION

During the 14th century, and the reign of Henry VIII (1509-1547), there were many changes that affected the lives of everyone in the land. Changes in religion but also, as a consequence of this, land ownership, and, thus often a change in local agricultural policy.

As King, Henry enjoyed hunting wildfowl in the area and regularly visited his friend Lord Rich (Lord of the Manor of Rochford) who served as Lord Chancellor of England from 1548 until 1551. They would visit Suttons, then known as Shoebury Hall, and shoot on the marshes there and in the channel. They also hunted together in the Royal Park at Rayleigh. Henry would also visit Rochford Hall, owned by Sir Thomas Boleyn, where he paid court to his daughter, Anne. At this time he was espoused to Catherine of Aragon, who he had married on his accession to the throne, but Catherine was now ailing and seemed unlikely to produce a male heir. His request to the Pope for a divorce so that he could wed Anne had been refused, so he married Anne in secret in January, 1533, five days before the English court that had been assembled specially for the purpose ruled his union with Catherine invalid. Rome refused to acknowledge the marriage and the result was a complete break from papal authority. In 1534 an Act of Parliament called the 'Act of Supremacy' declared Henry 'Supreme Head of the Church of England', anyone who denied him this title was deemed guilty of high treason. In return, the Pope excommunicated him from the Church of Rome and so began the dissolution of all the monasteries in England. Henry redistributed all the land and property previously held by the monasteries to chosen friends and associates.

Locally, his friend Lord Richard Rich (1496-1567) benefited greatly from lands taken back from the monks and his family became one of the biggest property owners in the Rochford Hundred. Among lands granted to him in 1537 were the title deeds and crown rights to Shoebury Hall and a pasture called Muschall Grange; with more land on the marshes this represented 'a tenth part of a knights fee'.

Ownership of the Hall passed down through the Rich family for several generations, the family adopting the title 'the Earls of Warwick'. Among them Robert, the second Earl (d. 1658), who was the Lord High Admiral and to his eldest son (another Robert) the third Earl, whose first wife was the daughter of Oliver Cromwell. By his second wife he had three daughters, the youngest, Essen (Lady Essex), married Daniel Finch, the Earl of Nottingham. After the death of Charles, the fourth Earl, there were no further male heirs, so in 1673 the Earl of Nottingham succeeded to the property 'in the right of his wife, Lady Essex'.

In the late 1600s he sold most of the Shoebury estate to the Bristow family, who had returned from America in 1680. An ancestor, Nicholas Bristow, had been clerk of the jewels to Henry VIII and his son, Edward VI.

Robert de Essex's Shoebury Hall built had been thatched. In 1568, after the death of Richard Rich, it was rebuilt and renamed South Shoebury Hall. Now the construction of the house was frame and Essex board, the entrance hall floor being made from cobbles brought over from Holland as ballast in a sailing barge.

It is recorded that Shoebury Hall was let to William Friend for 30 years, for a rent of £40.

In 1766 Thomas Parsons extended the house further by adding a further four rooms and two attics behind the original house. This wing was in red brick with large windows facing south. It is thought that the two storied part of the original, weatherboarded house must have needed the walls replacing at some time and that is why they are now built of yellow brick.

In the garden a round outbuilding of rustic red burr bricks was used for beekeeping; inside the wall are recesses that held the bee skeps. It appears to have been built just after the house was extended by Thomas Parsons.

LOCAL LANDMARKS

By now other buildings had appeared, including some that remain today, and very slowly others were added.

In the 16th century a new brick hall who built in the current Elizabethan style on the site of the old West Hall and became known as North Shoebury Hall. Some of the carved stonework from the demolished south aisle of St Mary's Church appears to have been used in the construction. In the early 18th century the first storey was weather-boarded.

In 1534 it is recorded that Edward Baber held 'Danger Fights'. Danger Hall (Farm) was at the junction of Ness Road and Elm Road in the vicinity of Vincent Crescent. It is reported as 'being much curtailed by the ravages of the sea' and is believed to be the site that Camden referred to in 1620 as 'a city, being swallowed up in the Maplin Sands'. The position so far inland makes this seem improbable but flooding, when it occurred, would cause overflowing of the tidal inlets extending inland from the direction of the North Sea by Friars Farm, and from large swells of water travelling along the River Shoe. Danger Farm was rebuilt in 1781.

The Reverend Philip Morant suggests in *The History and Antiquities of the county of Essex* of 1768 that Dangers Farm was formerly called 'Dawes'. However, a map of 1703 shows Dawes Farm to be where New Farm is today, just north of the railway bridge. It was once part of the estate of Kent's Manor, 'which crossed the boundary line of the two Shoeburys'.

Out on the marshes in a line north of the manor house Suttons two new farmhouses were built adjacent to each other. At this time it was a quiet, wooded area fringing the shoreline on the high road to Great Wakering. Frequented by many wild birds it was popular with hunters; the peewit, black and grey geese, teal and other wildfowl were in abundance. Cherry Tree Farmhouse was built first in

As it is today, the oldest wooden part of South Shoebury Hall

The Red (Brick) House

1568. This red brick building had inside a massive oak staircase with a trap door over the top, like that at Shore House, this could be lowered over the stairwell to block the ascent of unwelcome guests who might visit the isolated house. In 1584 Barnfleet Farmhouse (sometimes written Bamflete) was built.

In 1657 there is mention of Mountain Marshes, a portion of marshland belonging to Suttons. and later in the century Samuel's Farmhouse was rebuilt. Surrounding this farm was a moat connected by 'bourne' (stream) to the large lake 700 yards to the west at Bournes Green, the oldest known inhabited part of the area. Known as Eastern Mere this lake linked with a much larger Western Mere, of which the pond in Southchurch Park is all that remains today, both remnants of the large lagoon that once covered the whole area during the iron age. As the waters slowly evaporated over the years the area became very swampy, the resulting silt layer providing a rich source of brickearth for the building industry. The Samuel family had been local landowners since 1270, their farmlands being west of where Bishopsteignton is today.

When the Earl of Nottingham inherited the Rich family lands he began an extensive building programme. That year, 1673, the Red Brick House was built at the junctions of Shoebury High Street with Wakering Road, Elm Road and Blackgate Road. It was built as the lodge house for the manor house and stood at the entrance to the approach road leading to the manor, 'a beautiful avenue lined with trees that formed an archway overhead. A brick panel in the south gable bears the letters FR, with the letter M above, two hearts and the date 1673. The same insignia with the date 1681 appears on the weather vane of the manor house. These initials have been attributed to the builder, Francis Haydaston, and his wife Rebecca, who had died earlier in 1639. Another theory suggests they stand for 'Free Manorial Rights', indicating that the premises may have once been an inn granted 'rights' to sell alcohol and food. Several of the windows have at some time been blocked up, possibly as a result of the window tax imposed by William Pitt.

The house was used in more recent times to accommodate the gardener and steward of the manor, Mr Cooper.

The two farmhouses out on the marshes bordering the high road to Wakering were next for attention. First, in 1678, Cherry Tree Farmhouse was rebuilt, then two years later, it was the turn of Barnfleet Farmhouse.

In 1681, a little further south Sutton Hall was rebuilt and took the title Shoebury Manor, as South Shoebury Hall had adopted that title when it was rebuilt in 1568. It seems to have been smaller than its predecessor as the moat now extended well beyond the house. Now it was used as the Manor House, the manorial courts were held here instead of at South Shoebury Hall, but in the 1800s when they were transferred back again. In 1828, nearly a hundred and fifty years after it was built, the weathervane was found in the cellar and re-erected on the house, which by then was known just as Suttons.

In 1689 Chapman's House and Lodge were built, adjacent to the newly built manor house.

In 1722 Crouchman's farm was registered in the name of John Lodwick of Bamflete Farm. Access to it was around the marshland in front of Bamflete Farm until this inconvenience was remedied. It included lands on the marshes known as 'Barns' or 'Marshalls' and remained in the Lodwick family until it was sold in 1833.

South Shoebury Hall Cottages were built for the farm workers in 1724.

In 1730 Door's Farm was named after a tenant, Daniel Doors who died in 1768. Married to Mary Neal, he was a shopkeeper and village constable as well as a farmer. His son Samuel, who died in 1766, aged 25 years, was clerk at both village churches. The farm is recorded as being situated in North and South Shoebury and it is said that a highwayman who once lived in the house came home wounded from an encounter and died there. No doubt this was the same Dawe's Farm.

Star House and Star Cottages were in Star Field on the corner of Poynter's and Star Lanes. Star Cottages were on record in 1703, Star House was built around 1753 and was once licensed as a public house. Records show it was last licensed in 1785, although the cellar and wine bins still existed in 1906. Demolished in recent times they had been incorporated into Hutley's Farm for some time.

An old barn at the turn of the road leading from Poynter's Lane to Great Wakering was converted into a row of cottages, known as Mustard Hall or Barnhouses. In 1759 Peter Lodwick married the widow of Robert Kennett from Barnhouses, who had died the previous year, aged 45 years. The 'bride to be' rode behind Peter to church on a pillion 'along the narrow lane where the rooks built in the large trees'.

In 1763 a large barn built in 1500 on North Shoebury Hall Farm was meticulously re-constructed according to the instructions given by the owner, Christopher Parsons. He stated that none of the original timbers was to be used unless it had been specifically marked for that purpose, and the agreed price of £57 was to include £1 for taking down the old barn and selling off the timber for lathes. Mr Bowes, the carpenter, was assigned certain growing trees to use, which he and his men had to cut, hew and saw during the month of November, leaving the wood to season for two months; by Midsummer's Day all the wooden part of barn was to be completed. The finished barn consisted of three separate sections; an enormous storage area for hay and straw, a granary, and a protruding porch. The doors were built large enough to allow a loaded cart to pass through. Although keeping to his part of the arrangement, Mr Bowes had to wait nearly a year for payment, including the agreed £1.11.6d for finishing the job properly. The barn was in service for two hundred years.

Benton's Farmhouse was built in 1768 on the marshes near to Well House. After the government bought the land it was used as the Royal Engineers' offices and workshops.

The wooden framed building of Shoebury Cross House at Parson's Corner, North Shoebury, built in the 18th century, was weatherboarded with two gabled wings to the southern side. It served for many years as the post office, shop and blacksmith's forge.

In 1787 the White House on North Shoebury Road, first known as Barbour's, was rebuilt by Edward Kennett.

In 1796 the original Friars Farmhouse was built in the High Street. Farms on the coast used barges as well as road carts to carry goods and supplies, and an inlet of water running inland from Pig's Bay allowed barges to travel up to the farm to load cattle and hay. When the tide was in it completely blocked the roadway so people wanting to travel beyond to Suttons (now called King's after John King, the occupant), or to Wakering had to go in a roundabout way via Dangers Farm and back to the Red (Brick) House. The next year Woodbine Cottages were built by John King and in 1801 three cottages were built off the High Street: these were demolished when the Government put in the tramway to the new Ranges.

In 1824 on the site of the old Kent's Manor in North Shoebury Road Samuel Benton built the Moated House. Part of the moat on the southern and western side of the house was filled in and the new, smaller building was built closer to the water. The Fenchurch Street railway line now cuts across the original land, part of which was described as an osier ground. Fine osier (willow) branches were cut as canes and were traditionally used in making baskets'. The house was also known at one time as the 'gated house' because of the unusual barn-like building at the entrance by the moat.

North Shoebury House had a timber-framed wing added at the rear in the 17th or 18th century.

In 1825 a coastguard station and lookout, with accommodation for the officers, was built to the south of Rampart Street on the site of the old signal station.

In St Andrew's Church there is a memorial window depicting St Andrew and St Peter in memoriam to the first coastguard officer, Robert Melbourne, Commander Royal Navy, who died aged 37 years.

In 1829 John Knapping had Well Marsh Cottage (later Well House) built for his steward. Cattle would be brought to drink at the nearby pond from Benton's Farm, South Shoebury Farm, Danger Farm and Friars Farm. The charge was a ha'penny a head, per week. Dale Knapping took it over on his grandfather's death in 1833, and twenty years later the dilapidated thatch roof was replaced by galvanised iron.

In 1832 quarters to house twenty of the coastguards were built off the High Street in what would later become John Street. Also this year Mr Jones built Rampart Tavern. Frequented by the coastguards, local fishermen and labourers it was no more than a large black wooden hut until 1846 when it was altered to a large square room. During the evenings Mr Stafford entertained the patrons on his violin.

Having been sold by the Lodwick family, Crouchman's Farm was then tenanted by Samuel Poynter from Nayland, from 1833 until his death in 1886 at the age of 84 years. During this time, on 11th July, 1864, the farm premises burnt down. For many years he was a churchwarden and Poynter's Lane is named after him. In 1897 the farm was sold to Arthur Mills Kelmsley, who was among the first pioneers of the market garden industry in Essex and used a large part of the farm for this purpose, building nurseries on the land. He subscribed to the restoration of both North Shoebury and Great Wakering churches and other religious causes.

A second, smaller residence called Little Crouchmans, was built nearby in 1910 for the use of his second daughter and her husband.

The thatched Alderwalk Cottages were built in 1840 in a small lane off Elm Road: they were pulled down in 1896. Nearby Shuffey Row was built eight years later with tiled roofs and there was also a row of dwellings belonging to the brickfields called Earth Pit Cottages: nearby was Brickfield Farm.

In 1849 another establishment called the 'Men Found Out Inn' opened for business somewhere opposite the Shoebury Tavern. Philip Benton refers to an inn of this name in his notes, recorded as standing opposite an old isolated barn on Rampart Farm that was reputedly used for smuggling. According to Benton this farm belonged at one time to a Mr and Mrs Turner and stood 'against the barrack wall'. (This is confirmed by the Tithe Map for South Shoebury of 1849 which records Mrs Turner as owning several fields, one called Barn Field and another Beacon Field, no doubt the site of the beacon post that was lit to warn of invasion during the Dutch Wars).

H King bought it from the Turners and later the farm belonged to Dale Knapping 'who sold part of the land to the Government for the barracks, and built a thriving village on the remainder', undoubtedly Rampart Street, George Street, John Street and Dane Street.

From Benton's notes: 'Excavations suggested there had once been a river bed, indicated by the discover several feet deep of reeds and flags... leading from the waterworks to the lane by the Men Found Out Inn'. But in 1848 the Board of Ordnance had purchased the land known as the Ness and preparations began for its use.

LIFE IN THE PARISHES

Apart from those who worked in the large houses and on the estates the main employment was on the land, meagre wages being supplemented by catching rabbits, wild fowl and fish to feed the families.

The local parishes had always relied heavily on the church, the local lord and the charity of the more affluent in society for gifts and bequests to help the poor. Sometimes this provision, known as alms, was by way of food or money, or gifts in kind, although sometimes properties were donated to the parish to house them.

During the reign of Elizabeth efforts were made to solve the problem by encouraging parishes to take responsibility for their poor and to this end a 'poor rate' was levied for the first time in 1597 to assist in keeping the paupers of each parish. This often caused great hardship to those on whom the burden now fell, often very poor themselves, and there was much resentment that they were often supporting strangers who arrived, seemingly only searching for the best handouts available. The law was revised many times to find a suitable solution, allowing for only those people born in the parish to qualify for assistance; anyone else seeming likely to need help was quickly moved on. People who moved from town to town would be classed as vagrants and flogged.

In 1662 Charles II passed the 'Settlement Law' to try and persuade people not to move around from parish to parish. George III passed a law forbidding dole to be paid to wanderers who had not been whipped, flogged or imprisoned for seven days first: if they produced a certificate of flogging they could then claim dole.

Crime in the Rochford Hundred was high. Poaching, smuggling and wrecking along the coast were commonplace. Smuggling had been rife since the 14th century and continued until 1860. The highwayman, Dick Turpin, executed in 1739, was known to have engaged in smuggling here. On country roads footpads and highwaymen preyed on lone travellers, so people joined together in small groups for protection. Farmers employed armed guards when travelling the roads with their hay, produce or animals.

Every hamlet had its own stocks and whipping post to deal with offenders, but no pillory is recorded locally. At Shoebury the stocks were in a field at Parson's Corner, North Shoebury, opposite the blacksmith's shop at 'the three wont way', near the manorial pond.

A map of Shoebury Hall surveyed by John Watts in 1703 names the field as 'Motts', after the Motte family whose name appears at the time of Henry IV.

The stocks were used to punish drunkards and less serious offenders or to detain people awaiting trial, but most had disappeared from the scene by 1830. Those from the lower classes found guilty of petty larceny and vagrancy were usually dealt with by public flogging. Young offenders were spared this harsh treatment, but were beaten instead with a bundle of birch twigs, a form of punishment not abolished until the 1930s. Women who 'scolded' (passed on venereal disease) were ducked, usually in the local pond by 'ducking stool.'

The nearest gallows were at Barling until the late 18th century, sited near Mucking Hall, but under a ruling in the local manorial charter dating from the 11th century women were only executed by drowning until the 16th century.

From 1060 onwards there was a jail, with a nearby farm called Jail Farm. As late as the 1950s locals can recall prisoners working in the fields at Barling; these were not from the local gaol, but had been brought by bus from Chelmsford Prison to work on the land.

FARMING

By the mid-16th century, with the manorial system in decay, sheep farming was the mainstay under the new system of landlord farmers, with cattle being kept mainly for domestic use to provide milk and dairy products for the household.

With many Flemish weavers now living in small English villages to escape Spanish dominance at home there was no shortage of customers for the wool produced here.

After a visit to Essex in 1594 John Norden, the Elizabethan topographer, gave these report of the area in his *Description of Essex*, '...most fatt frutefull, and full of profitable things exceding (as farr as I can finde) anie other shire, for the general comodeties, and the plentie... this shire seemeth to me to deserve this title of the englishe Goshen, the fattest of the Lande; compared to Palestina, that flowed with milke and hunnye'.

Of the Rochford Hundred he wrote, '...milke, butter, and cheese in admirable abboundance; and in those partes are the great and huge cheeses made, wondred at for their massivnes and thicknes'.

In 1607 much the same opinion was expressed by another topographer who visited the area. William Camden, Headmaster of Westminster School, wrote of the Dengie Hundred north of the River Crouch, 'plentifull in grasse, and rich in Cattaille, but Sheepe especially where all their doing is in making of Cheese; and there shall ye have men take the women's office in hand and milke Ewes; whence those huge thicke Cheeses are made that are vented and sould not onely into all parts of England, but into forraign nations also, for the rusticall people, labourers, and handicraftes men to fill their bellies, and feed upon'.

In 1794 the local area was described, '...as near, if not nearer, perfection than in any other part of Essex. The land is in general of a deep, rich, tender, loamy quality, and as in other parts, rather farmed than grazed. The crops of wheat, beans, oats, coleseed or rape, mustard, and in short of anything that is sown, afford a great return'.

A widespread epidemic of bovine fever in the 18th century meant most of the cattle in the county were lost.

CLIMATE

The extensive marshy lands where the sheep thrived provided a poor environment for the people living there. Although Norden was impressed with the abundance of the area, of the climate he was less enthusiastic, 'I can not comende the healthfulness of it. And especiallie nere the sea coastes, Rochford, Dengie, Tendring Hundredes and other lowe places about the creekes, which gave me a most cruell quarterne fever'.

Marsh Fever, probably malaria, was quite common and was not eradicated until the mid-1800s. Women seem to have been more susceptible to the disease than men. Commenting in 1722 about the survival rate of the young women brought into these coastal fringes as brides for local men Daniel Defoe said, 'the young lassies... were healthy, fresh and clear, and well, but when they came out of their native air into the marshes among the fogs and damps, there they presently changd their complexion, got an ague or two... and died.' Some farmers are reputed to have outlived a dozen wives, over the river one man it is claimed lost twenty-five wives, his son, aged thirty-five, lost fourteen.

PUBLIC RECORDS AND MEMORANDUMS

Between 1529/36 Sir William Stafford, a squire at Rochford married to Mary Boleyn, was appointed commissioner to sell off many of the parishes' church bells, those of St Andrew's among them. The proceeds raised at auction were to be used for the benefit of each parish: it is known that at Foulness the money was used to repair the seawall, but some doubt was expressed as to the whereabouts of other receipts. It was suspected that they probably disappeared into the pockets of the local landowners.

In 1538 the Secretary of State, Thomas Cromwell, ordered that parish registers should be kept. This was so poorly adhered to that in 1597 the Crown ordered that public records should be compiled retrospectively from the beginning of Elizabeth's reign in 1558. In spite of this we only have records for North Shoebury from 1680, and South Shoebury from 1704. Shoebury is recorded in 1564/5 as having one ship, one master and four crew.

In 1578 Queen Elizabeth granted a lease to John Celye, a valet of the scullery, of a parcel of land called Munginge Marsh in North Showberye. After his death, owing to disputes among relatives, the property split up.

Maps show that at this time all roads passed through Rayleigh, the main market town and early centre of local government. Prittlewell was known as a 'sometyme market town'.

A LOCAL LITERARY

In 1548, during the reign of Edward VI, a new prayer book was authorised, the *First Book of Common Prayer*. It was mostly well received by the people with the exception of those who still regretted the break from the Church of Rome, and some continental Protestants who felt the reforms were not far reaching enough.

In 1580, during the reign of Edward's half-sister, Elizabeth, the incumbent at St Andrew's Church was the scholar and writer, Arthur Dent, an ardent follower of the new prayer book. Many of his sermons, 'written especially for the comfort of Protestants and the daunting of Papists, Seminary Priests and all that cursed rabble', were published in several editions as they were so popular.

He had been presented to his position at St Andrew's by Lord Robert Rich, of Rochford Hall, and would on occasions go over to the Hall to deliver a sermon there. When he did not arrive one day as arranged, Lord Rich asked his domestic chaplain, Robert Wright, who had been ordained in Antwerp, to stand in for him. In his address Wright referred irreverently to the local clergy as 'a pack of dumb dogs'. News of this outrage soon spread and his congregation quickly grew, swelled by many from the surrounding parishes intrigued by his outspoken manner of preaching.

The offended clergy, including Arthur Dent, lobbied against Wright and, determined to have him deposed, petitioned the Secretary of State. However, Lord Rich and his uncle approached the Bishop and appealed that Wright should be allowed to remain. The furore that resulted at this meeting, which ended in fisticuffs, came to the attention of the Queen, who ordered both Lord Rich and Robert Wright to be imprisoned. After the trial they were allowed free only on the condition that in future they adhered strictly to the teachings laid down in the new common prayer book.

During his stay at Shoebury Dent published a story, *The Plaine Man's Pathway to Heaven*, the tale of a man's journey from this world to the next related as a conversation between four people. When it was published in 1601 it was so popular that by 1637 twenty-four editions had been produced, by 1831 this had risen to forty-one editions. It is accepted by literary experts that this book was the inspiration for John Bunyan's story *Life and death of Mr Badman*, and to have strongly influenced his writing of *Pilgrim's Progress*, although his biblical mode of expression differed from that of Dent. On writing about his marriage Bunyan said, 'This woman and I came together as poor as poor might be, not having so much household stuff as a dish or a spoon betwixt us both. As her sole marriage portion she had brought with her two books, one of which was *The Plaine Man's Pathway to Heaven*, in these I would sometimes read with her'.

Although an intellectual man Dent was always mindful of his less sophisticated parishioners. One year, to celebrate 'fair day', a visiting preacher came down from Cambridge. His sermon was so full of learning' it was totally unsuitable for the rural congregation, mainly local farming folk. Taking him outside Dent showed him the hoes, flails and pitchforks set out for sale there and asked him what he would think 'if London jewellers or goldsmiths should come thither thinking to utter their diamonds or rubies or silver ewers'.

'Twould be absurd', the scholar replied.

'Just so with your Cambridge ware, the next time you come to my parish bring shovels and spades and plain truths', Dent admonished him.

JUSTICE
In the Civil Court
In 1563 a North Shoebury mariner and an Epping yeoman, who with others unknown had 'riotously made silent affray on Henry Baker of Canewdon and two

boys in the coastland marshlands, called Grapnelles, Gardens and Aye marshes in Paglesham and Little Wakering', were fined 2/6d. and were also ordered to pay 27s legal costs.

1588 John Bridge of North Shoebury 'did lay violent hands on the minister, William Hayward'. For what reason we are not told!

1601 Three gentlemen from North Shoebury, Henry Baker, John Baker and Peter Shakerley were arrested by John Sames for holding with swords and daggers the house of John Valentine, yeoman at Ulting.

1604 It is recorded that Henry Baker of North Shoebury had not paid his loan.

The last local trial for witchcraft was at South Fambridge in 1750. A couple were tried by the water ordeal which, according to custom, determined guilt by whether the accused sank or floated after being thrown into the water. In this instance the man was acquitted and the woman deemed guilty.

On 19th March, 1772, Thomas Drew's kettles (fishing kiddles) on the manor of North Shoebury were damaged. Joseph Hunwick exposed the culprit on 1st August.

The last death sentence for sheep stealing was at Southend in 1820 when two Prittlewell men, Henry Gilliot and Thomas Fairhead, were hanged for stealing a sheep. Both were aged 23, one a shepherd, the other a butcher. Gilliot had been married only one month, Fairhead's fiancée died from grief Another butcher from Wakering, Henry Jay, aged 21 years, was transported for life.

In the Church Court

In 1554 North Shoebury's rector is recorded as being deprived of his living for being married. This was restored when he separated from his spouse and did penance.

In 1566 the wife of Robert Hawks, vicar of North Shoebury, was accused of 'burning' (the term for passing on venereal disease) William Steven, and he to answer for 'incontinence with her'. Whether this lady was the wife of the above gentleman is not recorded, and how she acquired the ability to 'burn' remains a matter for conjecture.

A year earlier, the rector of South Shoebury, Thomas Martyndall, was a 'dicer and carder whereby he lost this Christmas £3'. Whether this was his stake money or his Christmas bonus we are not told.

The Lawless, or Whispering Court

The tenant at West Hall, North Shoebury, had to attend this annual court, so called because it was held at such an unlawful hour and was conducted in whispers.

Its origin is the source of much controversy. Tradition says that it began at Rayleigh, but was transferred, in the 17th century, to a house near the Stambridge Road, Rochford, purely for the convenience of the second Earl of Warwick.

A post with a spiked top representing a candle flame was erected in 1867 to identify the house. It bore the letters K H for Kings Hill.

Supposedly a lord of the manor, returning home one dark night after a long absence, had overheard his tenants in rebellious conversation. As punishment all those who owed him suit were made to gather at cockcrow each year on the Wednesday following Michaelmas Day to pay their dues at Kings Hill. Each tenant had to kneel and do homage in the dark, no lights were allowed or pens and paper. Forbidden to speak loudly they had to conduct their business only in whispers. The steward marked their name with charcoal on a post to signify their attendance, anyone not attending had to forfeit double his rent for every hour he was absent.

This procedure was first described in 1631, but it was never a court as we know it and over the years this became merely a formality for collecting rents. The custom eventually died out and rents were paid at a more conventional hour, but the court continued until the end of the 19th century and became purely a social function.

DEFENCE

Ship Money

On 4th August, 1635, Charles I ordered a levy known as 'ship money' to refinance the navy; its collection was met with much resistance. From Essex he required £8,000. Some large towns had separate assessments, while the balance was to be raised between the 'hundreds'. The total for this area was £308/1s/0d. The contribution for North Shoebury was £6/10s/0d, having 17 people assessed; for South Shoebury with 18 people being accounted for it was £6. Land was a contributing factor in deciding the amount.

Invasion alerts

In 1624 there was a false alarm, but a second alert in 1667, during the Second Dutch War, occurred when the Netherlands fleet, under Admiral Michael de Ruyter, sailed into the Thames. His burning of Sheerness and seizure of the warships lying there caused panic that next he would turn his attention here. One brigade of the Essex Militia was deployed from Hadleigh to Shoebury and beacons were lit as warning to prepare the district, but after a few minor skirmishes further up river peace once more resumed. The Dutch Vice-Admiral's ship was grounded off Shoebury.

In 1672 Charles II paid a visit to the Nore Buoy to witness trials of a ship called the *Greyhound* and the next year the English fleet gathered off Shoebury before sailing to fight in the three final battles of the war off the coast of Holland.

Trinity House asked for naval assistance to set the Shoe Beacon to afford better security for our warships as the estuary remained on full alert while hostilities continued. The following year things settled down once more when the Dutch William, Prince of Orange, and his wife, Mary, took the throne without any hostilities ensuing.

The Moated House, today simply known as the Moat House

Upturned broom branches were used as markers to show the course of the pathway, giving their name to the 'Broomway'

Fear of invasion grew once more during the Napoleonic Wars in 1798. Along with Foulness and Great Wakering, Shoebury was chosen to be a signal station. A manned station was built on the site later to be chosen as the first coastguard-station (now the Officers' Mess). This was used to communicate with Sheerness, and relayed messages to Lord Nelson's flagship when it lay anchored offshore at the Nore with a battle squadron charged with defending the Thames Estuary against any invasion force.

After the Battle of Trafalgar the damaged H.M.S. *Victory* once more anchored offshore before sailing on to Chatham Dockyard for repairs and refitting.

THE EAST COAST

The large expanse of the Maplin Sands, thirty square miles of mudflats lying directly off the east coast of Shoebury, was to play a vital rôle in the later development of the area. Over the centuries the sands had claimed the lives of many an unwary traveller attempting to cross them by the roadway from Wakering Stairs to the Fisherman's Head on Foulness Island, which was only accessible when exposed at low tide.

Laid on a base of Kentish ragstone this roadway ran parallel with the coast a quarter of a mile offshore, linked to it at intervals by headways. It is thought the Romans may have built the road, although the sharp inwards turn towards the coast at the Fisherman's Head is not characteristic of straight, Roman roads. One theory suggests that the original road probably extended beyond the present point, tapering inland more gradually, and that the sharp turn in was probably just another of the side feeder roads into the longer main road.

In mists and fogs the shoreline soon became invisible and the fast incoming tide, swirling around the path from either side, confused travellers as to which was the shore side. A great number of them wandered off course in the wrong direction on to the treacherous sands, 'certain death' as Mrs Knapping recorded in her writings much later on: 'From Sullons Headway, which leads on to the Maplin Sands and was used as a roadway to Foulness Island, turning to the left, one passes over grounds that often contributed waifs and strays to fill the churchyard at South Shoebury. The sea sent up its dead and many a nameless stranger found his last resting place here. A man named Snagsby some 200 years ago, walking up towards Shelford Head, leading to Foulness Island, lost the track on the sands and bearing too much to the left was drawn or fell into a quicksand where he disappeared for ever, the place where he perished being called Snagsby Hole, and wayfarers were cautious after that not to go too near the edge of the creek where the hole was said to be in existence'.

The Broomway is shown on John Norden's map of 1594. One area of these tidal mud flats off the New Ranges is known as 'The Black Grounds'.

The Maplin Sands are a rich source of the common cockle - at one time it was estimated there were over 1 million to the acre, providing a large proportion of the nation's supply.

Further west around the headland in the more sheltered water of the River Thames the sandy coastline was well suited for producing fine oysters. This provided a new industry in 1700 when it was noticed that a number of small oysters that had been tossed overboard into the sea off Southchurch at the end of a sailing journey were discovered still lying there a year later. Further inspection showed that these oysters had grown considerably since being deposited. They had thrived on the nutrients from the microscopic plant and animal life (diatims and foraminifers) in the water. The fisherman, Joseph Outing, took out leases along part of the foreshore and oyster nurseries became a new enterprise, gradually expanding westwards along the shoreline as far as Hadleigh.

More of the small oysters were needed so extra supplies were collected during the spring, mainly from Sussex and Dorset, and brought to Essex to be 'grown on' for the rest of the year. Although the shallows provided a warm environment for the oyster they were also left exposed at low tide and were susceptible to frost.

Rival fishermen from Kent, upset by this new competition threatening their livelihood, arrived one day intent upon destroying the beds. They were repelled by no more than a hearty rendition of the Riot Act, read from the Essex shoreline.

This area of estuaries and low-lying east coast experienced excessive flooding in 1099, 1236, and 1376-7. In the 15th century there appears to have been some respite, but on 25th January, 1552, Edward VI wrote, 'Of late there hath been such a tide heire as hath overflowen al medowes and marshes. All th'isle of Dogges, al Plumstead marshe, al Sheppey, Foulnes in Essex, and the sea cost was quite drowned. We hear that it hath done no lesse harm in Flandres, Holland and Zellaund, but much more. For towness and cities have ben their droune'.

Nearly two hundred years later, on 16th February, 1736, it is recorded, 'A general inundation coverd all the marshes and lowlands in Kent, Essex, Suffolk, Norfolk and Lincolnshire, and some thousands of cattle were destroy'd, with several of their owners in endeavouring to save them. The tide being brought in by a strong wind at North West was the highest of any for 135 years past.... The little isles of Candy (Canvey) and Fowlnesse, on the coast of Essex, were quoite under water, not a hoof was saved thereon, and the inhabitants were taken from the upper parts of their houses in boats'.

In 1800, an *Account of the Tides between Shoeburyness and Clacton*, prepared by the maritime surveyor to the Admiralty stated, 'The tides appear to be most of all affected by a sudden shift of wind from the southward to a strong gale in the north west quarter, which raises the tides to a very great and sometimes an alarming height, breaks down the sea walls and overflows and damages the lowlands: and sometimes causes two high waters in the space of a few hours'.

Storms off the coast, with heavy mists and fogs and cruel east winds, claimed many lives from shipwrecks and those who lost their way along the shore. The crew of the *Port Mahoud*, a 'man of war' from Leigh, were cast away in a storm, the boat oversetting and were taken up on this shore and buried here on 9th September, 1716. They were Thomas Gardner, Lieutenant; William Bowles, Quartermaster; George Cousgue, Quartergunner, all from Deal in Kent; Thomas Harris, Surgeon from London; John Ramster, Cook from London; John Coolings, Common Seaman.

In 1735 a very bad flood overwhelmed the land. Six years later it was reported 'Be it a warning ever hereafter, the Revd. Mr Silke came down from London in a Hoy commanded by a man named Wiggins, and by help of a boat, was put on the West Knock Sands'. These sands are two miles from the main land. The gentleman was a stranger to the area and in the darkness, it was scarcely possible for him to find his way, the area being intersected with swinns or creeks, and in one of these, during high tide, it is believed he perished. If the tide did not flow 'tis scarce possible for a stranger to come safe ashore'.

In 1751 John Staines were buried, died with cold on the shore, while on 1st November, 1755, a severe earth tremor shook the whole area, followed by a thick fog for eight days.

Six years after young fisherman from Foulness, Henry Hockett aged 20, was driven ashore here in his boat and tumbled overboard. His body was not discovered for two weeks, when found it was not recognisable being 'much eaten by fish'. Only his pocketbook that had survived unscathed identified him.

There are many such entries recording bodies washed ashore and many strangers are buried in the churchyard, all enquiries about them having proved fruitless. Some remained unknown, others were identified as having fallen overboard from passing ships; in 1739 one perished from the frost.

MEMORANDUM FROM THE PARISH RECORDS

Expenses

For conveying paupers to their own parish; Private intelligence	5s.3d
In 1766 there was a smallpox epidemic;	
Carrying a boy to pest house	2s.6d
charges there	£6. 1s.0d
For his family with smallpox Cage had given to others	£4.19s.7d
	£10.14s.7d
Carrying a man and his family to Thriplow, Cambridgeshire	£10.10s.0d
For burying a man on the beach at South Shoebury	1s.6d
1769 for coach and hire to Buckingham and back	£5. 7s.3d
For victuals and drink	£3. 4s.0d
For dame Mathews and children to Totham	£5. 0s.0d
gave her	10s.0d
fetching her back	£1. 0s.0d

In 1761 and 1768 small sums were given to the children in the workhouse to go to Wakering Fair.

In 1726 the rateable value of North Shoebury was £517.

In 1761 it was £549, South Shoebury £533 and Foulness £2,545.

Foulness was to contribute 40s to the workhouse, and both Shoeburys 25s

Monthly meetings were to be held and absent officers were to be fined 10s.

From the church registers of St Andrew's

1717 10 June. The minister and inhabitants beat the bounds of the Parish. This was an annual custom to walk the perimeter of the parish boundary.

1745 Joseph Willey of North Shoebury and Margaret Rogers (widow of her third husband) were married.

No stable was found at the parsonage and an entire new stable was erected 'at ye expense of ye rector, Mr Imber'.

1748 There is a strange entry among the burials, it reads, 'Wife of Thomas Waklin here died and buried in 'Fowlness'. And for ye journey two horses and a servant, and for the fees of burial and a funeral service offered 10/-. Let him be set by, and his 10/- perish'.

1764 A burial entry from North Shoebury reads;

'John Dimond, a reputed good fiddler, had drunk too freely and fell into a ditch by the roadside from whence he had scrambled out, but ye weather very cold and he wet, 'tis believed he perish V by those means, lay five hours perishing and was found in the road just expiring'. He was buried on 11th March, a verdict of accidental death was recorded.

South Shoebury Cottages

Chapter 4
THE GARRISON ARRIVES

The wide, marshy fields and unproductive heath land of the Ness area, coupled with the large expanse of mudflats off the coast made this the ideal location for its new, unfolding rôle. The Maplin Sands offered the necessary length of fire for testing and, for economy, shells could be retrieved at low tide for examination and possible reuse. Spasmodic visits had been made to the area since 1805, when experimental firing trials were permitted from the Ness on to screen targets placed out on the mudflats. It had previously been accepted that these tests included those of a new shell invented by Henry Shrapnel, but this theory is now disputed. Shrapnel's revolutionary idea of a shell that would explode bullets on impact was over twenty years old before the British Army finally adopted it.

The Napoleonic wars ended in 1815. Other trials took place at intervals, but it eventually became evident that a new permanent testing range was necessary, as the original site at Plumstead Marshes, so conveniently near to Woolwich Arsenal, was increasingly becoming a hazard, not only to passing shipping in the Thames, but also to the adjoining hay fields which were suffering frequent ignitions from the firings.

So it was in April, 1849, that the Board of Ordnance purchased land at the 'Ness' to set up a new testing range at Shoebury.

That summer the first signs of activity became apparent with the arrival of nine sappers and a sergeant, under their officer Lt A A Fisher. Their task was to set up the first gun battery emplacements, the sheds and stores, and make arrangements for accommodation in preparation for the future arrivals of men and horses. Lt Fisher allocated himself accommodation in one of the vacant coastguard cottages. His men lived in tents nearby, occasionally enjoying the luxury of a room at the coastguard station if one was available, until the following year when the 'old Sappers Quarters' were completed providing accommodation for twelve men.

Another year on, in 1851, the station became operational for experimental work with six men under Colonel E Welford. At first testing was confined to the summer months, the soldiers coming from Woolwich for just a few months a year. But building continued and by the following year there were many new buildings including a canteen and the wooden barrack blocks known as the 'black huts', ready to accommodate 200 men. Kirk & Parry, the company that built some of the accommodation blocks, later built the railway line extension from Southend to Shoebury.

Officers who did not want to suffer the draughty accommodation offered in the old coastguard block sought lodgings locally, or in Southend if they could afford the livery stable charges to take them there and back. The Royal Hotel housed several officers and their wives and families.

The Main Gate to the Garrison
The West Gate

Although ideal for sheep grazing the bleak marshland, with the cold east winds that frequently blew in from the North Sea, the Ness was not a popular posting for the first soldiers to arrive. Locals still pursued snipe and woodcock there, as they had done in the days of Canute and Henry VIII, and the whole area was over-run by an enormous rabbit population. These were pursued by the wild cats and dogs that roamed the area, there were so many cats that no one appears to have missed the presence of the number required to provide one soldier with a new hearthrug of a very furry nature.

With only a tiny rural population of 160 people and a distinct lack of local entertainment, apart from the two small taverns, Shoebury did nothing to endear itself to the new visitors. For any sort of entertainment they faced an unwelcome journey over unmade roads to Southend, four miles away. In spite of this setback the artillery men from the garrison soon became a familiar sight about the town, frequenting the theatres and bars there. The 'Halfway House', aptly named, provided a welcome watering hole halfway along the often dusty, sometimes water-logged road.

With the start of the Crimean War in 1854 practice work increased and for the first time the station was worked throughout the winter. A new post was created, Superintendent of Experiments, and Colonel J W Mitchell was appointed. It was around this time the first of a series of landing piers was built, near to the quick firing battery.

In 1855 the two rooms on the upper floor of the coastguard station which had served for three years as the Officers' Mess was granted recognition as an official offshoot of the Woolwich Mess and was granted the luxury of a servant. Over the following years the number of men and facilities continued to expand.

In 1856 the hospital was built with six wards, a surgery, storeroom, kitchen and a wash house at the rear. Also at the rear was an isolation block (itch ward) and dead house (mortuary). Work on the road through the barracks linking the Main (east) Gate entrance in the High Street to the West Gate entrance at the Grove was started. It was also agreed this year by the Secretary of State for War, Lord Panmure, that valuable lessons could be learned not only from the results of the testing, but from others observing the experimental work being carried out. Therefore a school should be arranged at Shoebury for this purpose.

In 1858 the volume of experimental work increased as the new rifled ordnance was introduced. Comparative tests between the Armstrong and Whitworth designs of the new rifled, breech loading guns proved them to be 57 times quicker than the old muzzle loading, cannon type guns. The smooth bore, 32 pounders that Lt. Fisher had set up platforms for in 1849 were now to be replaced by the new breed.

On 1st April, 1859, three years after the first decision was made, the School of Gunnery was opened. A fire station, stables, drill shed and eight further barrack blocks were added, but still men arriving for instruction had to be housed in tents

The Clock Tower in Chapel Road, built 1861-2

The black huts

erected in a field to the north of the barracks because there was no other accommodation available.

The long high wall from Rampart Street to the 'rookery' (near to the Customs and Excise building) was completed. A new residence was built at the end of Bridal Lane for the sergeant-major of experiments as that built on the beach at the common was deemed too draughty. This was known as the Caretaker's Cottage, or The Lodge. On the 'Ness', Barge Pier was built to assist with the movement of equipment by sea.

The following year it was necessary to install a hydraulic gantry as the size and weight of guns increased to withstand the shock of firing, pulleys and manpower were now insufficient to manoeuvre them. Before the power cranes were introduced sheers and hoists were used, the method being the same used to build the pyramids

In 1860 more land was purchased from the Bristow estate. With 180 troops now living in the black huts and over 800 building contractors working on the site for George Smith & Sons and the other contractors, there was a growing need to provide some sort of recreational facilities and evening entertainment for the men.

The '60s expansion saw more emphasis on this and the cricket field, tennis courts and a temporary theatre were established. The cricket field wicket was reinforced with a base of builder's rubble one foot deep, covered by target screens. Chestnut and sycamore trees were planted along two sides, trees still remained on the west and south side from the old Danish encampment.

Water services were laid on for the garrison in October, 1860, a supply tank was installed on brick supports alongside Grove Walk with a small cottage at the foot. The village people also benefited from this service until the start of the public supply.

In August, 1867, the garrison started its own gas supply with the gas works and coke store set against the perimeter wall adjoining the camp field. Gas Cottage once stood where the grassy mound is at the end of the long wall near the old rookery.

Among the improvements made in 1869 was a new clock tower, built because complaints were received that no one ever knew the correct time. It seems the concussion from the firings damaged the officers' watches, which they were still using to record the 'times of flight'. The 'black huts' were converted to married quarters this year and single storey married quarters were completed flanking the hospital four years later.

As more space was now needed to build officers' quarters in Warrior Square, the Royal Engineers moved their operations out to the marshes in 1875, taking over farm buildings for their machine shops and carpenters' shops that had once belonged to Benton's Farm.

By now the 'Horseshoe Barracks' was more or less complete, although it was not formally called this until 1940. The name was derived from the unique formation of the accommodation blocks in a horseshoe shape around the parade ground.

The 81 ton Infant

The barge *Gog* unloading an 111 ton gun in 1888; the rail line extended directly into the barge. Laying close by is the *Katherine*, which towed *Gog* to and from Woolwich

The War Department had acquired over 200 acres of land, meeting with fierce local opposition to gaining rights to areas of the Maplin Sands, especially from local fishermen, and had to face litigation in the High Court before it succeeded in proving its title. Today the Ministry of Defence owns two and a half miles of local coastline.

TESTING & TARGETS, THE BATTLE AGAINST ARMOUR PLATE

Since the advent of iron-clad warships the increasing thickness of the armour plate used in their construction meant that the size of guns were constantly having to be made larger to be effective against them. Experimental work increased around this time on producing more powerful projectiles to combat the newer, thicker plate - targets had been quite unsophisticated, sometimes just squares marked out on the sand or wooden screens, but now more elaborate targets were devised.

Three 5 inch steel plates bolted together were used as a representation of H.M.S. *Warrior* in 1860 to test a 300 lb shell. Another was of rolled iron 8 inches thick, backed by 18 inches of teak and a further 3 inches of iron, this was penetrated by the shell from a 9 inch muzzle loader.

A model of Plymouth Fort made of solid steel plates 15 inches thick was used for practice in 1868 by a 12 inch gun, another target was a representation of 6 French cavalrymen mounted on barrels pulled along by horses.

Much later, in 1892, 'running' targets were introduced. These measured 18 feet by 4 feet and were towed on either small-wheeled trolleys across the sands or by boats when the tide was in. They were pulled by a system of wires passing around bollards out on the range wound in by engines on shore. This allowed barrages of fire by four guns firing simultaneously at the variable speed targets.

A BIG BORE

A series of these muzzle-loading guns were produced, known as 'Woolwich Infants', so-called because of the care and tenderness lavished on them and the cradles used to transport them. In 1876 another arrived, the 'Terrible Infant', much larger than its earlier siblings. One shot thrown from the mouth equalled the firepower of 74 guns from a ship in Nelson's time.

Vital statistics: The gun weighed 81 tons, the carriage 40 tons. Barrel: 24 feet long, diameter 24" with a 14.5" (later 16") bore. Shells: 1258 lbs (later 1,760 lbs). Muzzle velocity 1,393 feet per second. Gunpowder charge: 370 lbs (this was enclosed in a silk bag, then a zinc box).

This extremely large and noisy 'baby' was loaded on its twelve-wheeled carriage into a barge for the journey from Woolwich to Shoebury. The barge *Magog*, specially built at a cost of £1,000 to carry the monster, was equally an enigma measuring 87 feet in length. Lashed down by cables, the 81 ton gun nestled in the 5' 6" hold ready for the journey to Shoebury where, in spite of heavy fog, it arrived safely. When it was eventually fired on the beach in front of the black huts, the whole town knew of its existence. An abbreviated report from the time states: 'A bugle sounded, a flag was run up, and there was a backward movement in the crowd of soldiers and sightseers. A second bugle sounded, the fuse was lighted by electricity, and an instant after the shot burst forth from the mouth of the gun with a deafening roar, accompanied by a volume of flame and a cloud of smoke while the ground shook as if moved by an earthquake. Away went the ball, in eleven seconds it had sped nearly three miles without touching the ground. After it fell it bounded along the sand far beyond the four mile course which had been marked out by the Royal Engineers, into the waves beyond, casting up a huge wave of sand and water in its progress. The second shot struck the ground half a mile away but continued on 8 or 9 miles into deep water. The third alighted at about 4 miles, then proceeded to make a trough in the sand 27 feet long, 13 feet wide and 9 feet deep before racing into the sea. The 81 ton gun and its carriage were hurled back along the rails over thirty feet, twenty of which were up a steep incline, notwithstanding that the brakes were put on the wheels to make recoil as slight as possible. The roofs on the nearby 'black huts' lifted a little from the blast'.

The inhabitants of the village of Shoebury did not admire this noisy 'infant' one bit for their windows were shattered to atoms. Plate glass shop windows cracked from top to bottom, the plaster showered down from the ceilings and walls of the houses and doors burst from their hinges, even locks were broken from the concussion produced by the discharge. The fact that the government would foot the bill was not everything.

The report claimed that the balls travelled faster than sound, the projectiles were in fact rifled shells. This first test of the experimental model in front of the black huts was for length of range and accuracy of trajectory. The following January the gun was moved to the Ness for trials against plate, the target used on this occasion was a representation of Spithead Fort. The screen of two 9" iron plates with a layer of teak between was penetrated by the shell which continued on straight through the granite blocks behind and into the concrete backing to a depth of 6", but not reaching the teak backing behind that.

Also this year the first production model fired. Guns would go back and forth to Woolwich for changes to the bore size and other necessary modifications, sometimes after only one test firing. In total eight of these 81 ton guns were produced: the test model, four for the ship *Inflexible*, two for the Admiralty pier turret at Dover, and one held in reserve.

Until telephones were installed in 1882, semaphore had been used to communicate between positions on the ranges. Now a cable was laid out across the sands and cut at intervals for the insertion of a telephone so that direct communication could be made with men working out on the range. Radio was not introduced until 1902.

The married quarters in Hospital Road (built 1876) in 1906

Michael's Cottages in Richmond Avenue, built by M Simpson

The first range lines at Hilly Marsh were up to 6,000 feet long, but with the increasing size and velocity of the guns longer ranges were now needed. This was not a practical possibility so near to the entrance of the river so yet more land was purchased in 1888 to create new ranges north of the village.

Within the old ranges standard gauge rail lines had sufficed until now with loads dragged by men or horses, steam engines were not in use until 1886/7. In 1888 work began on a full gauge railway track to be laid from the piers at the Ness to carry the increasingly heavy equipment to the exact sites where it was needed. This track was extended over the High Street by level crossing and a number of railway sheds from the garrison were re-assembled in Sutton's Yard ready for the trains that started running to the new ranges when the first battery became operational on 5th April, 1890. The 'old ranges' were now used only for accommodation and instructional work.

Now lying within the boundary of the new ranges, Chapman's House became the offices for the Experimental Department, with the stables, coach house and cart sheds of Sutton's utilised as gun sheds and stores until new ones could be built. The Royal Engineers took over Cherry Tree Farmhouse as their offices and used the farm sheds there for the blacksmiths and carpenters shops. They also used the yard at Sutton's.

During this period (1856-95) the Duke of Cambridge, a cousin of Queen Victoria, was Commander in Chief of the Army and as such he made frequent visits to observe trials in action. Many claim the Cambridge Town area is named so because of association with him - others attribute it to John Cambridge, the original developer.

In 1893 searchlights were installed to assist the guns should the need arise to use them at night in defence of the estuary: in 1900 they were electrified.

West Tower was built for the School of Gunnery (later the Coast Artillery School of Gunnery) to house the men and instruments that oversaw, monitored and directed the test firings. It was built at the old ranges near to the bridging pool that was used for practising construction of the floating bridges and cask rafts, needed to ferry equipment across the inlets on the marshy coast of the new ranges.

More married quarters were built in Campfield Road next to the Families Hospital in 1899, they were known as the 'Birdcage Quarters' because of the railings on the front balconies.

ENTERTAINMENT

During early spring, 1862, a meeting was held in the Officers' Mess when it was decided to run a variety entertainment during the winter months, with volunteers and locals taking part to put on sketches and concerts. Under the supervision of Captain Scott, the contractors erected a stage in the new drill shed. Sergeant McDonald and Bombardier Tupper worked during the summer painting canvas and skidding for scenery, and by November they were ready for the first concert to be given by the 'officers, ladies and noted families from outside'. The shed was very cold so it was proposed an entrance charge of 3d should be made during 1864/5 to raise funds for six stoves ready for the next winter.

AMATEUR THEATRICALS

The first stage play, *East Lynne* by Mrs Henry Wood, was performed by the School of Gunnery Amateur Dramatic Society in 1866 to a packed house, including the first army chaplain of the newly opened Garrison Church, Reverend Dudley Sommerville. During scenery changes the newly formed School of Gunnery Orchestra played selections of music. The Reverend Edward Bristow Wynne and Mr Alfred Webb lent their horse and traps to ferry people to the event, people came from as far afield as Rayleigh. Drag ropes were pegged down in front of the stables to tie the horses to, and rugs to keep them warm as they rested during the performance were provided by the Commandant.

The following year (67/68) began the first regular season of plays. The Commandant requested that the audience should not spend too long chatting with the grooms if they visited their horses during the interval, and to refrain from making a noise when returning to the drill shed if the play had already recommenced. The non-commissioned officers formed their own society this season, including some from the ranks, and from 1868 alternated with the officers in putting on plays.

Their first performance was *Diamond cut Diamond* and *Sent to the Tower*. For the first time tickets were issued, printed by Mr H Savage of Prittlewell Road at a cost of 50 for 4/6d. Seats could be reserved at Woosman's shop in Southend or at the post office for 3/-; tickets 'on the door' were 3d or 9d. This year also saw the addition of a 'coloured minstrel troupe'.

The entertainments were so popular that requests came from the Town Hall in Southend for performances to be put on there. The NCOs Society often appeared at the Public Hall in Alexandra Street, later known as the Rivoli and more recently the ABC cinema, and now once again being used a theatre. Many of the evenings of entertainment were put on to benefit local charities and needy residents.

During the packed performances given by the officers and ladies in July, 1884, the Reverend Alfred Malim, who had just arrived from Bermuda, was introduced to much applause. In September the new theatre, bought from the Healtheries Exhibition at Chelsea for £200, arrived in sections by rail and was carried to the site just inside the barrack gate chosen by the Commandant, Colonel Fox-Strangways. In November it was blown on to its side during a gale and work began again to re-erect it. December saw the last play presented in the drill shed. The Colonel said how sorry they were to leave where they had all spent so many happy evenings, but it was hoped they would be even happier in the newly fitted theatre which should be ready early in the new year.

PROGRAMME

of

CONCERT

to be given in the

DRILL SHED,

SHOEBURYNESS,

ON

TUESDAY 15th May, 1877.

Doors Open at 8, commence at 8 30.

Carriages may be ordered at 10.

ADMISSION: 2s, 9d, & 3d.

R. Will. HANBIDGE, Printer, Shoeburyness Garrison Press.

The dining room at the Officers' Mess   The stage at the Garrison Theatre

→ ❉ PROGRAMME ❉ ←

OF AN

ENTERTAINMENT

TO BE GIVEN IN THE

NEW GARRISON THEATRE,

BY LADIES AND OFFICERS OF SHOEBURYNESS,

(By permission of the Commandant,)

On TUESDAY, March 9th, 1886.

* *

DOORS OPEN AT 7·30.   COMMENCE AT 8.

Carriages may be ordered at 10.

Admission—Three Shillings, Ninepence, and Threepence,

Francis and Sons, Printers, Southend and Rochford.

Sadly, in March, 1885, Major J F Bally announced a cessation of theatricals for six months following the death of the Commandant, Colonel Fox-Strangways, in the dreadful explosion that took place on 26th February. Major Bally had been very fortunate to escape injury. He had been walking near the smith's shop close to the site of the explosiond; a flying splinter had struck him on his right side but he had been saved serious injury by a book carried in his side pocket that had taken the impact.

In August the first Shoebury Week was held, an idea proposed by the late Commandant Fox-Strangways.

The programme was as follows:

Sunday 10th	Church Parade
Monday 11th	Theatricals in the new theatre
Tuesday 12th	A dance at the officers mess
Wednesday 13th	A night treasure hunt, lit only by candles in jam jars.
Thursday 14th	An open air concert party on the cricket field with the Pierrot Troupe from London.
Friday 15th	A ball in the new theatre.
Saturday 16th	An evening band concert by the Royal Artillery Band. Farewell in the R A Mess.

A gymkhana, sports, tennis and cricket matches were held during the week.

The Ball was a huge success. A marquee holding 400 people borrowed from the Artillery Volunteers was erected in front of the Officers' Mess, the pathway between was screened by nine foot long targets and lit each side by magazine lanterns where the horses and traps of the visitors were parked.

An archway of flowers and flags led from the Long Course Officers' Quarters to the theatre, and the Woolwich Orchestra and Band played for the first time at Shoebury.

The ball lasted from 9 pm to 4 am. Decorations became more elaborate as the years went by. Dancing was held in the new dining room of the Officers' Mess when it was built, with the marquees then used for 'sitting out'. Electricity was supplied by battery to the strings of fairy lights that adorned the trees, and decorative ponds complete with miniature ducks and flowerbeds graced the marquees. Additions and variations appeared over the coming years; chinese lanterns became a regular feature, an indoor waterfall was installed, and some years the beach was used as the location for the buffet with the steps down to it carpeted, and the boathouse lit up.

In 1909 the new band stage was also illuminated for the week's activities. 11th December saw the official opening of the new theatre by the new Commandant's wife, Mrs Nairne. The society was renamed the Shoebury Amateur Dramatic Society and that evening's play was *Time will Tell*, chosen because it was a favourite reply of the Commandant's when asked anything, and the reply given when asked if he thought the new theatre would be a success. The proceeds of the two night's performances, totalling £35.12.6d, were donated to the Rev Malim towards the Garrison Church fund.

Raised platform seating was added the following year to the front of the gallery so that those sitting in the shilling seats could see more. The demand for tickets was so great that performances were often by invitation only and the local train times were changed to enable theatre-goers to catch the train home after the performance.

Band Concerts were also very popular. Visiting bands were entertained, and the Garrison band would perform at outside venues. Many of these were benefit performances to aid the local community.

The drill shed hosted evenings of readings from popular books. These dramatic renditions were usually supplemented with other variety acts.

The social life of the villagers and many further afield benefited greatly from events held within the garrison, but in 1893 a marked drop in attendance was the subject of a meeting held in the theatre by the Commandant to discover why. It appeared that since the introduction of the railway, and with Southend now only a 4d return train journey away, soldiers were seeking their entertainment elsewhere. Performances were cut to two a year, the NCOs disbanded their theatrical group and offered their assistance to the officers.

Between 1900 and 1902 there were no theatricals, as so many officers had left the station for the South African War. Occasional concert parties came to give a free show to the troops.

SPORT AND COMPETITIONS

The Garrison provided a full sporting programme and facilities for the men who worked there. Their teams played and participated in many fixtures with the civilian population. From 1873 an annual Aquatic Sports Day was introduced, and two boat teams, one of six oars and one of four competed in races from Shoebury to the pier.

Shoebury Gunners Football Team began as a result of the informal eight-a-side matches played between the troops and men from the contracting firms who were building the Garrison. The 'Gunners' team was one of the oldest teams in Essex, formed in 1871 after the Commandant, Colonel E Elwyn, had called a meeting at the drill shed to discuss the idea. The first team formed was from the School of Gunnery and No. 4 Battery of No. 1 Divisional Troop R.A. Early opponents were the employees of George Smith, the Middlesex Cinque Ports and the Essex Artillery Volunteers. After the railway was extended to Shoebury in 1884, they had a larger variety of teams to play, including Thames Ironworks (now West Ham). They first entered the Army Cup in 1892.

The Queen's Prize Firing Competition was started in 1865 and held annually for the volunteer soldiers of the National Association of Artillerymen. The

Water polo, 1890
Aquatic tug-of-war, 1906

competition became such a popular event it was extended to run for the last week in July and the first week in August. It was a most festive occasion as teams from all over the country - and some from as far away as Jersey, Guernsey and Canada - set up their tents on the camp field.

The large marquee was capable of holding 1,000 men, with a smaller one holding 400 used as the officers' mess. The camp even had a post office. The teams competed firing five rounds at the targets laid out on the mud at low tide, different times for completion were allowed for each class of gun (18, 24, 32, 40 or 64 pounders), and a point was deducted for every minute taken over the allotted time.

Disaster struck two years running when high winds blew away the targets, and one year there were red faces when it was discovered that Woolwich had not taken into account that new rifled shells were needed and not enough had been provided.

Nearly always, an important guest - a member of the Royal family or an army dignitary - attended for the prize giving ceremony that was held on the last Friday. It was a spectacular event with the trees festooned in flags and 200 people watching from the flag draped grandstand as the men marched past back to the camp with their coveted prizes. As well as the £100 Queen's Prize there were other donated awards. The public came from miles around in their horses and traps to listen as different bands played each evening outside the tented Officers' Mess. In five years the number of entrants had grown from 650 to 2,000. After 1899 competition ceased for the duration of the South African War, when it resumed again in 1904 Queen Victoria was dead and it was renamed the King's Prize.

The isolated location of Shoebury was not a poplar one, it did not attract the fashionable followers that many would have liked so now only the finals were held here. Then, after another break from 1914-1920 for the Great War, it was held just once more at Shoebury before it was moved to the Isle of Wight.

ACCIDENTS
For such a large undertaking of a dangerous nature accidents were relatively rare.

The first fatality was in September, 1854, after a 56 pounder burst, but the previous year eleven men had been seriously injured when a 32 pounder burst at the breech.

A volunteer artilleryman was crushed when a gun slipped from its carriage in August, 1880. Five years later a dreadful explosion occurred on the 26th February when things went badly wrong as tests were being carried out on a new delayed action percussion fuse. Having experienced difficulty inserting a fuse into the 6" shell of a breech-loading gun Gunner Robert Allen handed over the task to Sergeant-Major Sam Daykin.

As he tried gently tapping the fuse into position there was an explosion that resulted in seven fatalities and many seriously injured. Summoned immediately by

Captain F M Goold-Adams, Sgt-Maj Sam M Daykin, Colonel W A Fox-Stangways, Gr Robert Allen and Gr James Underwood, who died in the 1885 explosion

The Memorial Hospital

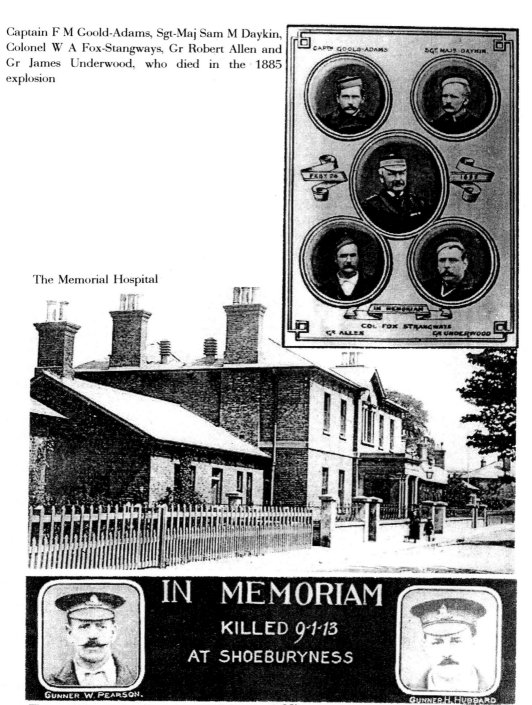

The two who died in January, 1913 (see page 93)

telegram four doctors rushed to the scene from Southend, a special train was put into service to take them there.

Gunner Allen was killed instantly, six others received dreadful injuries from which they later died. Among them the Commandant, Colonel Walter A Fox-Strangways who lost a foot and had both legs shattered. Despite his injuries he arranged for letters of sympathy to be sent to the bereaved families before he died.

Colonel Francis Lyons, the Superintendent of the Research Laboratory at Woolwich who had designed the fuse being tested also died after losing both legs. Also mortally wounded were Mr Frederick J Rance, a foreman examiner of fuses at Woolwich, Gunner James Underwood and Sergeant-Major Daykin.

The Assistant Superintendent of Experiments who was in charge of the group and leading the tests was Captain Francis Goold Adams who had only taken over the post two weeks previously. As he lay dying his wife, who had been standing nearby observing with their young child comforted him. Her first fiancé, Major M Lambert, had died two weeks before their planned wedding after falling into an icy pond and catching a chill on a February day in 1880. He had been a popular officer and churchwarden at St Andrew's, a memorial window depicting Pilgrim's Progress was installed in the north wall of the nave in his honour.

On 6th March the *Southend Standard* reported a longer account of the inquest. The late Commandant Fox-Strangways did not long survive the amputation of both legs by Sir William McCormach and died shortly after 6am on Friday morning. Colonel Lyon succumbed just before eight, about noon Gunner Underwood died. The Surgeon General W McKinnon later arrived to inspect the situation, the telegraph sent immediately after the accident from Mrs Fox-Strangways requesting his presence had gone astray, so Sir William had been wired for urgently to operate in his place.

The inquest was held at the Shoebury Tavern, before the coroner, Mr J Harrison. The 14 members of the jury were taken to view the bodies at the different locations. When viewing the Commandant it was noticed 'that the features of this most lamented officer wore a pleasant expression'. The inquest was adjourned for the official government enquiry and certificates of burial were issued.

Colonel Francis Lyons, aged 51, was buried in the family vault at Stretton, near Warrington. The Commandant, aged 52, was buried at Rewe, four miles from Exeter. Both men were given a military escort as their coffins were taken, on separate days, to the train station to make their last journey home. From the barracks to the railway station soldiers lined the route and a large crowd gathered to observe the processions. The firing party, consisting of two batteries, led the gun carriage drawn by six horses that bore the flag draped, oak coffins that were covered in flowers.

Behind followed the mourners and the School of Gunnery Band, which played the Dead March as they approached the station. After the formal farewells to the family members, soldiers lining the platform presented arms as the special trains steamed out of the station.

Mr James Rance, the artificer from the Royal Laboratory, was buried at Woolwich.

Four of the funerals took place at St Andrew's Church with over 3,000 troops attending. The procession was so long that the head of it, led by the Royal Engineers Band from Chatham and the Royal Artillery Band from Woolwich, had arrived at the church before the end had left the barracks.

First came the gun carriage drawn by four horses carrying Gunner James Underwood, it was attended by a firing party of one sergeant and thirteen gunners, the six pall bearers included two survivors of the blast. Behind came the family mourners.

Next to pass by was Gunner Robert Allen with a firing party numbering the same, his pallbearers included two survivors from a previous shell explosion six months earlier. His family followed behind.

Sergeant-Major Daykin's group followed, his firing party numbered 19 sergeants and corporals.

Lastly, with a firing party of 100 rank and file men, came the body of Captain Francis Goold Adams, carried on the carriage of one of the new 12lb guns he had been working on. As each body passed the officers saluted and the men presented arms.

The route was lined by a double row of artillerymen who lined the road inside the barracks, with mounted police and volunteers controlling the crowds around the church-yard. Thousands attended from as far afield as London. The whole of the district closed their businesses for the duration of the funeral. Today a memorial stands at the site of the accident, near to the battery in the old ranges.

To commemorate those who died in the tragedy the Memorial Hospital for Women was built in 1898 by donations raised from the public, the first matron being Miss E Bedingfield. It continued to be funded by voluntary donations until the government took it over in the early 1900s after it had almost been forced to close and had only managed to keep going for a further years through the efforts to raise funds from the theatre revenue. It was later renamed the Military Families' Hospital.

Discarded ordnance claimed several civilian victims. In 1855 two 16 year old boys were killed trying to carry away a shell, and in 1890 a 15 year old, Alexander Smith, died while playing with a 4" shell while on holiday.

For many years there were, fortunately, no more serious accidents.

Chapter 5
THE VICTORIAN ERA

The arrival and growth of the garrison had changed the lifestyle of Shoebury from a sleepy farming backwater to a busy town with an increasing population to serve the needs of the new inhabitants. Along with the spreading army establishment the civilian building expansion programme kept pace.

Until then there had been no village as such. Shoebury was still just fields and a few farms and large houses. The High Street had not yet been established; there was a private track over the fields with farm gates at intervals, over which the public had a right of way. The main route into Southend was along what is now Elm Road, then turning wither right at Dangers Farm passing North Shoebury Hall, St Mary's Church and Parsons Corner, or left towards the sea, past the lane leading to the old parsonage, then past South Shoebury Hall and on to the common and the road along the sea front.

By comparison, Benjamin Disraeli referred to Southend in 1833 as 'a row of houses called a town'. Twenty years later, just before the introduction of the railway, *Chambers's Journal* described Southend as 'consisting of one long strip of houses, a strange jumble of old mansions, cottages, shops, tarry boathouses and boat building sheds, fishermen's dwellings, hung over with nets, and public houses'.

However, once the railway line arrived the population began to expand rapidly, including many of the men who had come to the area to build the railway and who stayed on and brought their families to join them.

GROWTH BEGINS

With an increasing need for building materials, Dale Knapping had already established a small brickfield with four stalls and a wash mill behind the Manor House in 1840, at this time the pug mills were horse driven. Three moulders, Mr W Stafford, Mr Avery and Mr Knott were brought over from Kent to make the red bricks. The arrival of the army increased demand still further and by 1862 the number of brick making stalls had steadily grown. At first they were extended along the 'Shorefield' below the coastguard station, then more were added behind the Red House, and from there they continued to expand westwards along the north side of Elm Road as far as the site later to become the waterworks tower.

In 1872 engines began to be used in some wash mills and chain drives began to replace horses. The new 'Model B' Brickfield (where the Vanguard Way industrial site is today) with twelve stalls was opened in 1888 at the end of the High Street, so called because it used only the new chain driven machinery to the stalls instead of being purely manually operated. These chain drives were changed to shaft drives at Easter time, 1904.

The range of banks at East Beach was known as the 'ten range' because there

Local bargemen in 1869. Left to right, front row: S Howard, J Mead, T Outram, T White, R Hallams, J Howard, S Howard, Jnr, J Prow, W Bowman

East Beach brickfield. On the right, the trucks that took bricks to the barge jetties; Mr Gundy can be seen at the door of his upturned ketch home; on the left, Bell House

were ten holding banks for the marm, this field was in operation until after the first war.

From here the finished bricks were transported to the beach in trucks carried on two narrow gauge railway lines crossing the High Street at the junction of what is now the Goslings, and Gunners Road. There were no crossing gates, traffic just stopped when required to allow the trucks to cross.

A bell was rung to warn of approaching storms so that the bricks laid out to dry could be covered. Wet days meant the men could not work and had no pay, some would hawk fish around to earn a little extra.

Sailing barges carried away bricks not destined for local construction work, although many were used in the building of the Southend district and Leigh. The barges would sail right up to the beach jetties for loading.

Before the introduction of Portland Cement a form of hydraulic cement known as Septaria was made, which had been in use since Roman times. Where the 'London clay' soil met the shoreline and formed into low cliffs cement stones could be found below the surface, prodding with rods by the locals to locate the stones was later discouraged by landowners because of the damage it caused. These stones were collected and taken to a factory in Leigh to be processed. Small pieces were placed in a kiln with breeze and burned in the same way that chalk is burned to produce lime, they were then ground down finely, sifted and put into barrels to be later mixed with sand and water. Shoebury was one area where these stones were to be found. Chalk and clay used in the manufacture of Portland Cement was also plentiful in the area.

After years of little change to the farming families, the population of Shoebury was now altering dramatically. In 1861 the combined population of North and South Shoebury was 350, the majority being in the farming communities of North Shoebury. Within 10 years it had grown to 1,695 as the less productive heath area around the Ness fulfilled its new purpose. With the arrival of the artillery came opportunities for employment locally and the village itself now began to grow to accommodate the influx of labour.

New shops opened around the garrison gate to supply the needs of the new inhabitants, not only the soldiers but their families, who were now coming to join them. The shops and building trade flourished, the railway brought more employment and the local people filled the places in other service industries needed to support the expanding town.

THE VILLAGE SLOWLY GROWS INTO A TOWN
DIARY
1858   Dale Knapping bought back a small section of land from the Government at the bottom of Rampart Street, formerly Rampart Farm, to provide access to East Beach. Only here was unlimited public access allowed to the beach between George

Rampart Street

Shorefield House

Street and Blackgate Road. Access was permitted only when there was no firing in practice, as indicated by red flags flying.

Unlimited access must have later been denied as on 16th May, 1884, the *Southend Standard* reported: 'The right of way to Shoeburyness Beach... The much talked of chain and posts which were put up as a barrier at the end of Rampart Street to stop the right of way to the beach, and which have given rise to so much dissatisfaction, were, during Saturday night or Sunday morning, broken down; the chain has since lay on the ground.'

1858   Rampart Street and the High Street were made up by Dale Knapping

1859   Dane Street, John Street, George Street and Smith Street were made, the latter three streets taking their names from John and George Smith, the contractors. Six cottages were built, four of them in Dane Street and two in George Street, and Gothic Row (after the pointed Gothic style of the roof) was built in Smith Street.

The workmen's office was in John Street. In a small alleyway between John Street and the High Street, next to the quarters of the coastguard men and the office of Mr Hopkins, the clerk of works, a baker's shop was built to provide bread for the soldiers. This was to become known as Bakers Yard until the area was knocked down and rebuilt over one hundred years later. By then Mr Gillett, the first baker who came from Faversham, was long since forgotten.

1860   A working men's club for Knapping's employees was established in Dane Street.

1861   With the original coastguard station now enclosed within the newly established barrack perimeter a new station and lookout with staff housing was built behind Shoebury Common, where Thorpe Bay Yacht Club is today, and Bunter once guarded his well.

While excavations were being made for the footings of the new building human remains were found. The old station and the rebuilt quarters now became the Officers' Mess and were in use until recently.

1862   Shoebury had its first schoolroom known as Church, or Shoebury, School. Finished earlier in the year, it opened in August at the bottom of Hinguar Street, now the site of St Peter's Church. It was just one large room that also served as a village community centre and a chapel of ease to the parish church of St Andrew's. Until then it had been necessary for local children to travel to Wakering to attend the nearest school, so it was a great advantage for the local families. Dale Knapping and George Smith, the Pimlico contractor responsible for much of the local village and garrison building work, financed the project. Mr Knapping later purchased Mr Smith's financial interest.

A house, with its own orchard, was built for the first schoolmaster, Mr William Cox. Miss Eleanor Cox was the schoolmistress. The schoolroom, built to seat 200, had 158 pupils (83 boys and 75 girls), the room was enlarged in 1875 to accommodate another 75 children and a cloakroom and office added to meet the

Hinguar Street School
Mr Hillyer's class, 1921

requirements of the Education Department. Until 1878 when the general rates took over financial responsibility for the school it had been funded by the Knapping family, helped by educational grants, a subscription from the Reverend Edward Wynne and 'school pence'.

By 1886 the number of pupils had grown to 370 and the present Hinguar Street School was built. At first it took only infants and ran in tandem with the original school, but in 1903 a new junior block was added which allowed the whole school to be housed on one site.

Miss Tessie Grater was then schoolmistress, and Mr Millbank the attendance officer. After Mr Cox came Mr Hillyer, then Mr Deal and next Mr Dale: names still recalled today by older residents who recall the sternness of Mr Hillyer.

1867   Brampton House, some cottages and a new baker's shop owned by Mr Banyard were built in the High Street. All were demolished sixteen years later to make way for the new railway station. Behind Brampton House was a smithy. James Kirkwood took over the Shoebury Tavern.

1868   A boathouse to build barges for the increasing trade was built on East Beach at the end of Rampart Street. Five years later a second was needed. This year the old parsonage at the Grove was pulled down: the Government had bought the land and an officer's house was built there.

A new rectory was built to replace the parsonage on open land that would later become Ulster Avenue. The first vicar was the Reverend Edward Bristow Wynne.

Well Marsh Cottage in Ness Road was now known as Well House. In 1838 the Tithe Map recorded the owner as 'the poor of Shoebury'. The *Almanac* of 1872 recalls that it was at some time given to the parish by an unknown donor and let, with the garden next door, for £6.18s as the poor house. For many years it stood empty until a grateful young man, upon his marriage, accepted the chance to live there rent free, which he did for about twenty-five years. Sadly for him this state of affairs ended when, under the new Poor laws, he was required to pay a rent to the parish for the privilege of continuing to live there. After the government bought the land in 1870 he was paid five pounds to vacate the property.

Eight years later Major M Lambert had it pulled down and rebuilt, red tiles from Holland were put on the sides and roof. These roof tiles were replaced by slates by Major Hinde CRE in 1884.

This story was related by an old, eccentric tenant farmer from the Crispin family who lived at the nearby South Shoebury Hall. Although well to do he preferred to dress in the comfort of his old coat, which by all accounts consisted of so many patches of differing materials that it resembled a tailor's pattern sample, and boots that had little of the original remaining but the tops after twenty years mending. Nevertheless they were beloved by the owner 'like old harness to a saddler' and he greeted these boots with' the delight that one acquaintance greets another'. Observing his progress along a muddy road one day crying 'come up, come up' as he sat atop his rough legged nag, prodding it frequently in the ribs with his heels and umbrella, a friend was prompted to the greeting 'why here comes three kicks and a bang'.

The farmer's story relates to an orchard that belonged to the Hall near the pond. In an effort to catch the culprit who was stealing his apples he was creeping one moonlight night with his gun when he caught sight of someone sitting in a tree. On calling out to them 'down dropped a two legged creature and made for the Well House'. He fired at the intruder when he was a distance away and peppered his legs with shot before the thief jumped into and swam across the pond. The next day the culprit's wife arrived at the farm to report to the farmer that her husband had been taken very ill and needed a doctor - an ailment that apparently necessitated the removal of pellets before he could recover.

When the road was widened in the 1930s the old cottage was pulled down and a new house built further back.

1877   Mr George Alp built a blacksmith's shop near to the boathouses on East Beach. Also in 1877 Mr Bradley built the Cambridge Hotel (named after the Duke of Cambridge). The brewery, Courage, put in Mr Outram as manager, but then found they could not open because the new public house was not the statutory 'one mile distant' from the Shoebury Tavern. This inconvenient discrepancy was overcome by measuring the distance along the High Street to the Red Brick House, along Elm Road to Dangers Farm, and then to the 'Cambridge'. But it was two years before this ingenious solution allowed the hotel to open for business.

1878   Dale Knapping died in Paris, where he had spent much of his time. His body was brought home to be buried in St Andrew's churchyard.

Police Constable Smith, number 203 of the Essex Constabulary, took up his post as Shoebury's first constable.

1879   William Kirkwood took over the Shoebury Tavern after John died aged 55. The inn and gardens had become a popular meeting place for locals and visitors. There were twice-weekly dances in the evenings; coloured lights lit the gardens and by day there were shady corners to sit out in, and swings to relax on.

1883   Elm Cottages were built in Elm Road. On 18th February the new Salvation Army Hall was opened in Ness Road. Mr Tom Hills, Mr John Ayling and Mr Walter Green had taken services before they had a proper meeting place.

THE RAILWAY COMES TO SHOEBURY

Although the presence of The Royal Artillery had brought a vast increase in the local population (by 1881 it had increased by over 2,000 in forty years), the London, Tilbury, & Southend Railway had remained just that. The line had never been extended any further east since it had terminated at Southend in 1854.

The railway company were reluctant to venture further into the low populated, marshy area beyond Southend and the War Department had at first resisted the

Shoeburyness Station, 1907

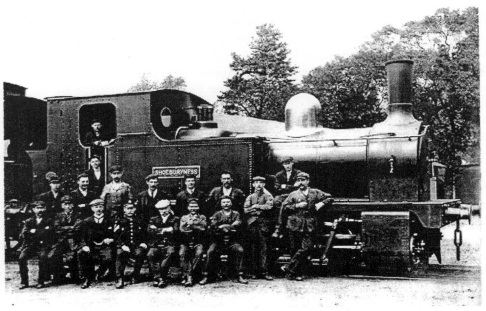

Royal Engineers' driver staff, 1904

idea of the railway being extended to Shoebury. Memories of continental invasion threats in the past made them wary of providing what appeared to be a fast route inland for any further, potential invaders. But the inconvenience of having to make the journey from Southend to Shoebury by cart over poor roads, sometimes almost impassable in inclement weather, and having to transport heavy equipment the same way, sometimes dragging it behind teams of horses, was becoming a source of real concern.

To help alleviate the problem Barge Pier was constructed on the Ness in 1859 to enable heavy ordnance, ammunition and other necessary materials to be brought in by sea and unloaded close to where they were needed. This sufficed for some time but eventually, after pressure from the War Office, it was agreed in October, 1882, that the railway line should now be extended. Without any tenders being sought the work commenced promptly by Kirk and Parry, building the line to the same schedule they were already using in Lincolnshire for the Sleaford to Spalding line. This company also did a lot of the construction work within the garrison.

There was some dissent from some local farmers and landowners whose land it would pass over, and much consternation was voiced over the plan to route the line across the High Street using a level crossing. This was the cheapest solution, with the line simply continuing on from where it had previously stopped. The objections to a level crossing were overcome by lowering the High Street by 18 feet to enable the tracks to be carried across it by a bridge.

On 1st February, 1884, the station was opened, the first train being the 7.15 am from Southend. Two days later 1,200 tickets were sold to passengers wishing to try the new service. Until Shoebury got its own loco shed the train had to come down from Southend to commence the first "up" service each day.

The railway was welcomed with open arms. The boom in carrier carts and the hackney carriage business waned. No one wanted to endure the long, uncomfortable journey or pay to have their kit transported any more.

There was a staff of four: Mr Beeton, stationmaster, Mr King, signalman, and Messrs Kirby and Crowhurst, the two porters.

1884 The Cambridge Town Estate now began to take shape with roads being established on land formerly belonging to South Shoebury Hall, seventy plots had been sold off at auction. West Road, St Andrew's Road, Sea View Road, Cambridge Road, and Grove Road (built on the grove of the old Parsonage) were gradually developed.

Father Muir was the first priest when a small square galvanised building became the first Roman Catholic Church in Ness Road.

There was now the start of definite divisions beginning within the small town as the Cambridge Estate began to take shape; the original farming population mainly to the north, now supplying produce to an ever increasing local market. The village community that had sprung up around the barracks, supporting the new enterprise and the business it generated. Now a new residential estate, effectively cut off from the village by the swathe of government owned land between, the only road at this time passed through the garrison.

1886   Church Street and Hinguar Street were made up, many of the cottages in Hinguar Street were built to accommodate the railway workers. The street was named after one of the early Danish invaders, 'Ingvar'. He bore the nickname 'Ingvar the boneless' because he was reputed to have sat in a melancholy state and gnawed his fingers to the bone when hearing the news of his father's death. The Anglo-Saxon Chronicles record that he and Hubba were the chief men of the army that killed St Edmund in 894.

Church Street was later renamed and became part of Hinguar Street. A proposed road to run from the station to the beach, parallel with George Street, to be called Wulfgar Street, after another Dane, was never built.

In 1888/90 it became necessary to provide a separate road to enable the civilian population to travel freely between the village and the 'Cambridge' without having to use the public right of way through the garrison.

A new road was established cutting across the camp field used to accommodate the overflow troops. This was achieved by opening a gap in the barrack wall at the end of Smith Street and effectively extending it to meet up again with the original road at the old Grove (opposite the entrance to Gunners Park). Thus the new road was aptly called 'Campfield Road'.

Work also began on Linton Road. York Ogden built Love Lane cottages in Shoebury Road.

1893   The Wesleyan Chapel capable of seating 250 people was built in the High Street (today the junction of Gunners Road) at a cost of £1,000. Gradually the new streets at both ends of the town began to fill as houses went up piecemeal.

1894 December saw the formation of the South Shoebury Urban District Council. The first meeting with nine members was on 2nd January the following year, a year that saw the streets on the Cambridge estate lit by oil lamps.

1896   The foundation stone was laid in Ness Road for Victoria Hall. Built by local builder A J Harris at a cost of £390, it was opened in 1901 as the Parish Hall. Accompanied by the School of Gunnery Band the opening ceremony was performed by the wife of Colonel J F Bally. Three years later the hall was enlarged. This stood where the entrance to the Towerfield factory estate is today.

In West Road, on the site now occupied by Sanders Store, the Peculiar People's new chapel was declared opened by Mr York Ogden.

In 1896, under the Public Health Act, the newly formed Council took over control from the private water company and work started that year on a new water tower and engineers cottage in Elm Road, then called Waterworks Lane, at a cost of £3,240. Water had always been drawn straight from individual wells scattered about the area until two years earlier in 1894, when water mains were first laid.

Then the first piped water came from the Rochford Union because at this time Southend could not assist with supplies. A new well was sunk in 1911 at a cost of £2,115; during the '30s water was obtained from the Thanet Sands strata.

1899 On 16th January, Rector Edward Causton's wife dug the first spadeful of earth to commence work on the new St Peter's Church in Dane Street. The Rector, who was unwell, watched from a closed carriage as his curate, the Reverend White, conducted the ceremony. On Easter Sunday the church opened and was dedicated by the Bishop of Colchester. Three years later in August it was relocated in the High Street at a cost of £210.18. 10d. The Methodist Chapel was built in St Andrew's Road.

Demolished by the brewers, the old Shoebury Tavern was replaced by the new Shoebury Hotel, Mr Pontoon was the landlord.

Council memorandum

1895 House refuse collection   £90 p.a.
Inspector of Nuisances salary   £25 p.a.
The Council's first General Rate 1/4d in the pound, reduced to 4d in the Autumn.
1896 Council expenditure was estimated at £1,483 for the next year and the rate raised to 1/9d. The first parish magazine was printed.
1897 The word 'South' is dropped from the Council's name.
1899 The Council drew the Rector's attention to the shallowness of some of the graves in the churchyard.
1900 A private company began building the new gas works in Elm Road.

THE THREE MANOR HOUSES

South Shoebury Hall having been bought by Robert Bristow in the 17th century along with the church living, remained in the family until 1866.

Philip Benton relates an interesting account of a fire at the Hall in 1861, it describes a scene of mayhem, worsened rather than helped by those called on to assist: 'A frightful fire took place upon South Shoebury Hall. It broke out about 11 o'clock at night and the whole of the buildings, with the exception of the house and a stack, fell sacrifice to the flames. Soon after the flames began to take a mastery, the soldiers, one and all to the amount of some hundreds, from the barracks, arrived at the scene'. It goes on to tell of the praiseworthy and successful endeavours of some to save a wheat stack by bodily removing it out of harm's way. How, while the tenant farmer, William Knapping, was busy directing operations to save his carts and implements, another group of soldiers went to the house, which was in no imminent danger.

In a time deemed to be shorter than that needed to tell it, 'locks were wrenched off, twenty dozen bottles of wine and liquor consumed, the panels of the doors smashed in, window frames forced out, large bed posts broken in half and the furniture thrown from the windows. Scarcely a piece remaining'. It seems the effects of the drink, including a bottle of train oil, caused some to run amok and into the fire, one was found in an adjoining field donning several shirts, and the scene next morning found 'the common strewn with spoils'. Much speculation abounded as to why it had happened, the few who were identified were reprimanded and those found with goods imprisoned by a civil court. The insurance company viewed it as 'damage done under a hasty removal'.

The Bristow family forebears had returned from America in 1680 and over several generations, mostly Roberts, a great deal of money and property had amassed. The family fortune was soon disposed of by the expensive habits of the last owner (yet another Robert), whose extravagant lifestyle soon depleted the plentiful coffers and forced him eventually to seek his living as a London taxi driver.

In 1866 the remaining assets were sold. A description of the Hall in the sale catalogue describes the Hall as: A comfortable residence, containing on the ground floor; entrance hall, dining and drawing rooms, two sitting rooms in the rear, kitchens, scullery, dairy, larder and cellar. On the first floor; two good bedchambers, and three other bedrooms at back approached by a separate staircase; on the upper floor two attics. The out offices comprise; stable for two horses, coach house, fowl house etc. adjoining on two good yards surrounded by new farm buildings consisting of a new barn, stabling cowhouses, horse shed, cart lodge, piggery etc. Also a cottage containing six rooms with yard, barn stable, cart shed etc.'.

The 'new' buildings mentioned were, no doubt, those erected to replace those demolished by the fire in 1861. Before the fire the barn and other outbuildings had formed the boundary of the manor yard, then the line of elm trees were enclosed within the boundary fence on the eastern side of the churchyard. As the barn doors opened directly on to the churchyard it was not an uncommon sight to see horses and machinery working there on the church land. Rebuilding work after the fire rectified this problem, and a new boundary fence was built leaving the elms within the Hall grounds. In 1863, and for several years after, a manorial court was held there.

As well as South Shoebury Hall, Dale Knapping purchased 'Suttons' from the Bristow estate, the house on the marshy coast overlooking the Maplin Sands. The Knapping family already tenanted both houses as farmers.

SUTTONS

This description of the property appeared in the sale catalogue; 'it is approached by the road through a beautiful avenue of trees. In front of the house is a small lawn and flower garden from which a flight of stone steps leads through a glazed portico to the hall panelled in oak, on one side of which was a moderate sized drawing room with walls in ornamented oak panels; on the other side, is a drawing room,

Suttons, fronted by a moat and the High Road to Wakering

The Coast Guard Station

also in oak. In the rear, a study and business room;... and the servants' offices, consisting of kitchen, scullery, larder, storeroom, apple room etc.. On the first floor, four good bedrooms and drawing room... and w.c. on half landing. On the second floor, five bedrooms. On the upper floor two attics. Basement, capital cellars.

The house was surrounded by a moat and a high, red brick wall that sloped down either side of the entrance making it clearly visible from the High Road that passed in front. Two bridges crossed the moat from the road and another crossed to the shore. In front was a common and marshes running along the shore to Wakering.

An underground passage is supposed to have led from the cellar to the shore, used to bring illicit cargo to the house. Another is rumoured to have run inland linking up with the Red Brick House. No evidence to support this was apparent to recent visitors to the house, but there appeared to be some subsidence to the surrounding wall at a point opposite the Red Brick House.

The grounds contained an orchard and gardens with a tulip tree to one side, and stables and a coach yard to the other. A stone mounting block assisted visitors to alight. Apricots, peach and fig trees grew there too. This house now took over from South Shoebury Hall as the Manor House.

In 1890, twelve years after Dale Knapping's death, it was sold to the government when more land for new ranges was needed. At this time the oak staircase with a heavy balustrade and oak panelling in the rooms either side of the entrance hall still remained, they were regarded as very fine and quite rare.

In the past the house had also been known as 'Kennets', and 'Kings', after the current families who occupied it.

In 1897 Mrs William Knapping wrote of the house, 'There is a large cellarage there, I fear me not always used in the old troublesome times for the storage of generous wine, though during the earlier portion of the present century it probably harboured many a keg of good Hollands, when the smuggling crews, aided by our rustics, made a successful run, as they often did pretty nearly, if not quite on to the forties.

'The twenties and thirties saw plenty of it, for many a good farmer in this district found, in the early morning, that one of his wagons, with a goodly array of stout horses, had been requisitioned during the night but, in addition, his stable furnished him with a handsome present of the aforementioned kegs so no questions were asked, no bulk searched for.

'The parish constable slumbered on beside his staff of office, and his glass of Hollands (hot or cold to taste) adding to his quiet home comforts; we leave him happy as we found him.

'Dare I say that our good parsons were not forgotten? Their generous parishioners would have scorned to run their cargoes under their very noses, not their eyes (for, by some chance or other, they might happen to be turned in some other direction at such times) without depositing some of those suggestive little kegs to warm them to their work of visiting the sick or sorry on those snowy winter nights, which their kindly hearts were ever ready to prompt them to do when needed

'And how about a scrimmage with the excise officers, and a wounded man or two; aye, wounded to death sometimes? Well, the parson was there with words and feelings suitable to the occasion. They were no shirkers, those manly gracious parsons of old, and so the old parsonage was not forgotten.

'Sir Robert Peel's force of able men had not even loomed in the distance, nor were they needed, and the parish constable dozed on in a thinly populated neighbourhood serenely conscious that he had done his duty by all.

'In the underground cellar was a large stone slab. What had it once hidden? Or what does it hide? Why was it there? Is it there still? I know not'.

NORTH SHOEBURY

In 1843 at the farm adjoining the Hall the Hutley family began training farming apprentices.

A local newspaper report for 7th December, 1883, read: 'The foundation stone of the new vicarage was laid on Tuesday afternoon, in the presence of several of the parishioners and other friends. The vicar, having first offered up prayer for the success of the undertaking, Mrs Wilmott then proceeded to lay the stone with the usual formalities. A jar containing a record of the proceedings, inscribed on parchment, a newspaper of the day, and some coins were placed under the stone'.

The item printed below this for the following day states: 'A Blue Moon: At about half past four on Wednesday afternoon, the moon presented an unwonted appearance, it being then of a distinct sky-blue colour'.

In 1885 St Mary's Church, North Shoebury, was restored with much assistance from the Benton family. They not only contributed financially but also oversaw the renovations, with Philip advising on the historical details and William acting as architect. Philip, junior, was the churchwarden.

Just north of St Mary's was 'High House', the workhouse that served Shoebury. Since Elizabeth had first attempted to address the problems of the poor and destitute in 1597, and standardize a national system for their care, many solutions had been tried over the years to alleviate the problem.

At times the old and sick were given monetary assistance or cared for in almshouses and poorhouses, and the able-bodied given work in the new workhouses set up by the parishes under a new law passed in 1723.

In 1782 parishes were permitted, should they wish, to amalgamate their workhouses with other parishes. Now they cared only for the old and infirm while the able bodied received assistance money known as the 'outdoor relief system' to take care of themselves.

The ever-increasing burden of the 'poor rate' was crippling to those forced to contribute to it and in time new remedies were required to dissuade those who happily relied on the parish to supplement their income. To remedy this problem a Royal Commission was set up in 1832 to investigate the Poor Law. The resultant Poor Law Amendment Act of 1834 did much to bring down the high costs of outdoor relief.

The new reforms now required several parishes to join together in 'unions' to provide more efficient, shared workhouses, this being more economical than each supporting its own establishment. The handing out of 'doles' of money and food, known as 'outdoor relief, was now to be stopped except to the old and sick. Any able-bodied person now seeking assistance was to be carefully vetted and admitted to the workhouse only if found eligible.

The restraints this imposed on the able bodied recipients now made it an unpopular option with far fewer people now wanting to apply for assistance. This in turn put pressure on their employers, the local farmers, to pay a reasonable wage. Until now they had been quite content to pay a mere pittance to their labourers, safe in the knowledge that the parish would supplement the wages of anyone requesting help. It also forced many who had relied on their 'dole' to supplement what they could earn themselves by their own produce, to move away from the land to more industrialized areas where they could earn a full living in the factories. It was also the death knell of many local cottage industries.

Built in 1763, High House now served as the workhouse for the parishes of North and South Shoebury, and Foulness. At this time all workhouses would have in charge a governor and sub-governor. The poor were obliged to wear a uniform, dark grey clothing with a badge bearing the letter 'P' and the first letter of the parish on the shoulder of the right sleeve, the women were also obliged to wear strong brown worsted stockings. Failure to comply with these rules meant 21 days in the house of correction.

The inmates were employed spinning worsted from 'locks' of wool bought from Suffolk, it was then reeled before being sold on to be dyed. It then went to the manufacturers of 'bays and says'. Records kept state that the spinning receipts for one year were £14. Spinning wheels cost 3/6d each, spindles 9d a half dozen.

The old workhouse building was burnt down on 14th September, 1877. It had previously managed to survive the severe gale in 1836 which had destroyed buildings and blown down many trees. A report of the fire in the *Southend Standard*, states, 'At 1.30 am on September 15th, a fire broke out in the Old Workhouse, North Shoebury, which belonged to Mr Parsons, North Shoebury Hall, and was let out in three tenements. The Royal Artillery fire brigade were quickly in attendance, but the building and furniture were all in a blaze before they could reach the spot; the fire was, however, quickly extinguished, but nearly everything was destroyed. Mr Parsons and only one of the tenants were insured.'

Nearby stood a small croft called the 'Pikle', or Pyghtle (the celtic word for a parcel of land), past which led a path to the church. This building was the old weaving cottage to the workhouse, later it was used as farm workers' cottages, then a private residence.

The last owners were the Misses May, who supplied blackberries and other produce to 'Greenfingers', the greengrocers in West Road. When it was vacated by them it fell into decay and was pulled down.

LIFE IN THE PARISHES

As an agricultural district the people of Shoebury were amongst the poorest; the land provided only seasonal work and many were without a living during the winter months. After several bad harvests between 1776 and 1802, things became even worse when, in 1806, Napoleon put a temporary blockade on trade between France and England. With no imports of grain, the price of wheat at home steadily increased. There was a rush to increase wheat production by clearing more land and draining marshy areas to provide larger open fields. Local farmers literally 'reaped the benefits' of this new era and their standard of living was greatly enhanced.

When the war ended, as a sop to landowners who feared a drop back to pre-war prices, new Corn Laws were introduced to keep price levels artificially high. No foreign imports were allowed unless English prices rose above the war-time £4 per quarter, effectively protecting the high price.

In 1830, with bread at prices they no longer could afford, and with concern growing over the reduction of land available for grazing their animals following the Enclosure Act, when much common land was taken and enclosed for farms, the people rose up against the government. The ensuing Swing Riots precipitated the review of the Poor Laws in 1832.

In 1836 farmers faced a fundamental change to the old system of rents. The Tythe Commutation Act ended the payment of 'tythes in kind' to landlords, and replaced them with a monetary rental. Maps were drawn to indicate the properties in each district and the scale of charges due to the landowner. The Tythe Map for South Shoebury is dated 1838, that for North Shoebury 1849.

By 1875 imports of cheap wheat from America were increasing thus causing the prices paid to local farmers for their wheat to fall. This caused ruin for many, some farms failed. Grain agriculture in the area declined rapidly and, with no market for the harvests, fields were left to revert to pasture. The Essex economy had relied heavily on its wheat yield.

The demand for fresh produce slowly began to increase as towns began to develop during the mid-19th century, there was also a need to supply them with milk and grain. The advent of the railway system now made the distribution of these perishable foods a commercial proposition. The markets of London were now accessible, quickly and easily reached by train, and the constantly increasing spread of the towns provided a ready market for locally grown produce. By the end of the century small market gardens had been developed to supply these new customers.

Sheep farming was still important, in Parliament the Woolsack was chosen as a symbol of the country's prosperity, its contents being considered one of England's finest assets.

The draining of marshy areas to provide more growing space for wheat during the early decades of the nineteenth century had resulted in a great improvement to people's health as the air quality became much improved but smallpox still remained common locally until vaccination was made available in 1818. Typhoid, cholera and diarrhoea continued to be a problem until the introduction of proper sewage facilities.

Opinions seemed to differ on the climate. On 15th February, 1833, Benjamin Disraeli wrote to his sister from Porters Grange: 'You could not have a softer clime or sunnier skies than at abused Southend.' But in her book *Only a clod*, Mary Elizabeth Braddon complained that Southend was exposed to 'the concentrated bleakness of perpetual east winds'.

On 22nd April, 1884, a tremor was recorded locally. The *Standard* of 25th April reported: 'The Earthquake... at the Royal Hotel and at several private houses along the seafront the bells rang and pictures, gaseliers, jugs etc. were set vibrating. At the Royals the walls rocked and people ran into the street in panic. At Shoebury it was severely felt, especially at the residences of Col Lewis and Dr Browne; at the former place the servants left the house in alarm'.

On 2 August, 1888, after an already wet July, 2.8 ins of rain fell causing flooding and disruption to rail services.

At the end of November, 1897, gale force winds and a high tide caused flooding mainly to the north of Shoebury. The children had to be taken to school by cart as the road from the Cambridge Estate was flooded and impassable on foot.

CRIME

Country roads were still little more than tracks, sometimes barely passable in winter and lone travellers were easy targets. People formed groups for their own protection, not wishing to rely on a justice that was haphazard in meting out justice to offenders.

Drunkenness and affrays were still common. This could increase in the summer months with the influx of visitors. In August, 1874, after two days of minor clashes, Southend police asked for assistance from the Shoebury garrison when, fuelled by alcohol, yet more fighting broke out between two groups of holiday-makers from the East End. Those not confined to the cells were sent on their way home.

Shoebury people came under the jurisdiction of the Rochford Court. In 1880 some hearings were held in Southend as well as Rochford at the insistence of

Southend traders who objected to travelling miles to Rochford. At last, in 1883, Southend finally got its own courthouse built in Alexandra Street.

BRICKMAKERS, BLACKSMITHS, BOATBUILDERS AND BARGEMEN

Many local men worked in the brickfields. Before mechanisation it was very heavy work, with most of the bricks being moved around by wheelbarrow.

During the winter local clay was cut and deposited at the wash mills for 'washing'. In these circular pits a turning wheel mixed the clay and water into a yellow consistency which was then drained off into the retaining marm banks. Rows of these enclosures appeared rather like giant ice cube trays, here the mixture was left until some of the water had evaporated leaving a much firmer substance called 'pug'. The surface of the mixture dried to a thick crust that appeared to be quite solid, but it claimed the life of one local boy who drowned when he attempted to walk across the surface.

When it was ready it was dug out by a pug boy and taken by barrow to be worked.

Each working stall had:

a temperer, who made sure the supply was constant and of the right consistency.

a flatterwak, to cut the pug to the approximate shape of the mould.

a moulder, who placed it in the mould, trimmed it and then put the finished brick on the shelf to be taken and loaded by the barrow loader.

The 'pusher out' took them to the offbearer who set them up on rows of racks to dry off. If it rained they were covered over by wooden roofs called 'atcaps'. After the drying process the 'crowder' ran the bricks to the kiln where they were fired in large kilns.

In 1861 they were working from 4 am to 8 pm to produce 50,000 bricks a week. One moulder, Mr Knott, could handle 900 bricks an hour. When the garrison was under construction men would transfer the bricks from the fields to the site by barrow, for this they earned 1/- a day.

Right on the beach itself, below Rampart Terrace, was the blacksmith's shop, built by George Alp as a repair shop for the barges being built next door. The building burnt down after 20 years and was replaced. About the time it was rebuilt Mr Sawkins took over as blacksmith, as well as working on the barges, he would shoe horses. Such was the demand that it was not uncommon before the 1914/18 war for horses to wait for two hours on the beach before being attended to.

Next door was the boat-house built by Mr Cook. The barges constructed here were made mainly for the local brickfield owners but some were made for customers as far away as Burnham.

Mr Rose, from Brightlingsea, arrived to take up his work in Shoebury by taking the ferry to Wallasea and walking the rest of the way via Potton Island and Wakering. He had been a shipwright in the Merchant Service during the Crimean

Mr Gundy, known by local children as 'Mr Punch'

Mr Gundy's home, the upturned ketch on East Beach. Behind are the brickfield offices and the manager's house, Bell House

War and his old sea chest was part of the furnishings. One story he related was of an order for a motor boat placed with him just prior to the onset of war. Nothing was seen again of the man until four years later when, the war over, he returned unannounced to enquire after the making of the boat. There, to his surprise, it was waiting for him, ready for the sea.

During the heyday of boat building six shipwrights were employed and as many as five or six boats would be hauled up onto the beach waiting to be worked on. Mr Rose's sons followed him and the business grew to building bawleys for the Leigh cockle and shrimp industries, pleasure yachts and motor boats.

The river was the main artery for trade and conveying goods before a reliable road system was established. The barges that came to collect the bricks did not come empty laden. Among the many cargoes they carried was sewage and horse manure, brought down from London for use as fertiliser by the local farmers, and beer for the Shoebury Tavern. There were wheeled jetties on the beach for loading and unloading the barges that sailed right up the shore.

Some of the barges were the *Kathleen*, owned by Mr Millbank, the *Rover* and *East Kent*, owned by Mr Stafford, the *Ness*, *Coxion*, *Shorn* and *Six Sisters* owned by Mr Cook, and Dale Knapping's barge *Effort*. The *Shoebury*, built by Mr Rose in 1879 for Mr Cook, could carry 50,000 bricks; its skipper, Mr J Howard, later bought it. The barge *Scud* held 46,000 bricks.

In 1893 an insurance claim was lodged against Mr Millbank by the owner of the barge *George and Susannah*, after it was in collision with his barge *Kathleen*.

	£	s......	d
Value of *George and Susannah* as valued			
by Wm. Hall, Bargebuilder, Paglesham	450	0	0
Value of cargo of bricks	47	5	0
Freight on board	6	15	0
Value of captain's clothes and personal			
possessions lost in barge	19	17	0
Ditto mate's	2	17	3
Loss of time	3	0	0
	£529	14	3

Mr Millbank made a counterclaim for his losses in the incident.

Dale Knapping had brought to East Beach an upturned ketch as a store house for boat tackle and equipment, for several years Mr Gundy used it as his home. He is reputed to have once swum from Tilbury to Gravesend in chains for a bet.

The officers had never experienced any problems being accepted here, being willingly entertained by the local gentry and dignitaries at social gatherings and croquet matches on garden lawns, but the common soldier met for a long time with prejudice and distrust. In time they too became accepted, some married into local families and became a part of the community. This was a dramatic change for a small population that had experienced little outside influence for centuries.

The School of Gunnery, 1884. Back row, third from right the Presbyterian Minister, extreme right Captain Francis Goold-Adams. Front row, second from left Rev A Malim, centre Colonel Walter Fox-Strangways

Volunteers marching through High Street from Station to Barracks, 1902

Disdain was now reserved for the newest visitors to arrive, the day-trippers to Southend. Their noisy arrival by train and steamer upset the peace and quiet previously enjoyed by the residents of the town.

Lt A A Fisher was the officer in charge of the first party of sappers to arrive in Shoebury that summer morning in 1849 to prepare for the coming army presence. He was very athletic, a keen runner, soon recognised in the district as he pursued his activity. He also set up a tennis court and entertained as his guests, Dale Knapping, Captain Baldwin, the coastguard officer, the Rev Wynne York and the Rev James Montagu. If a fourth was required, Sapper Donaldson obliged. Lt Fisher married Carry, the daughter of the Rector of St Clement's, Leigh.

During the Opium Wars, ten years after his arrival in Shoebury, he earned his ribbon as Chevalier de la Legion d'Honneur when he distinguished himself in the action to take the Peiho Forts. When he died twenty years later, from the malaria he had contracted in China, he had reached the rank of Colonel.

The Reverend Montagu was the curate at Sutton Hall and relished the company the new visitors to Shoebury afforded him. He met Lt Fisher soon after his arrival and was delighted to accept an invitation to dine in his quarters at the old coastguard station. Referring to this later he would jokingly claim to have been the first guest to dine at the Officers' Mess, as Lt Fisher's old rooms later became. Before the garrison had its own church this reverend gentleman would come over to conduct the services held in a barrack block in the black huts. He would happily collect shopping lists from the families and the following Sunday brought their groceries with him in his trap.

He relished the activities of the garrison and witnessed the first firing of the Woolwich Infant, noting that those that stood behind felt very little effect from the ignition explosion, whilst those who stood at right angles were rendered partially deaf. On one occasion his pet dog was scampering about on the beach when firing was in progress and was caught in the leg by a piece of 'elm sabot'. Carried on a sack to the hospital the projecting article was thought to be his bone and 'shooting Ginger' seemed the only option. Luckily, the offending item was recognised and removed enabling Ginger to hop back to a full recovery. Visitors from the barracks attending the Rochford meet would often call in on him. Once he had to trim off the muddy hems of the ladies dresses after they had trailed, ravenously hungry, across a ploughed field hoping for refreshment at his home.

Reverend Philip Wynne York was another well-known local figure who enjoyed the sophisticated company the garrison introduced. An accomplished amateur whip he enjoyed driving out around the district in his coach and four, often accompanied by a group of 'his fighting men'. A favourite outing was to Rayleigh for dinner.

He was the last occupant to live in the old parsonage at the Grove. This description appears in Benton's notes: 'A picturesque place was the old Rectory at the time the Revd Philip York was incumbent of the Parish, with its thatched roof

The new Rectory

The White House

and odd nooks and crannies and corners and its grand old master, kindly squire and parson in one, driving his coach and four greys himself. Such beautiful animals they were too, in which he took so much pride, for Revd York and his splendid turnout were admired the country round for many miles. With no resident squire, he fulfilled the double duty to his small and humble flock - personal attendance and spiritual help for the sick soul, invalid nourishment and the medicine so much needed in this malarial district - quinine and port wine to the poor and wasting body were freely given by the kind pastor and friend.'

The need for special medicines (port wine and quinine) lessened as more trees were cut down in this thickly wooded area and more land drained, reducing the dampness arising from decaying leaves, undergrowth and stagnant water; gradually the marsh fever disappeared.

Couples going to register the banns for their marriage always entered by the carriage driveway at the front, but left again by the rear entrance, for this reason it became known as the Bridal Lane.

It was a condition of the tenancy that tenants were required to plant osiers (willows) there to maintain the woods. In front of the Rectory was a small stream called the Heronry. Rights to hawk and fish there were granted to South Shoebury Hall and Dangers as late as 1863. 'This stream takes its course through the marsh dykes to the Great Sluice where it falls into the sea' (probably the waterway in Gunners Park). The Reverend Philip York died in 1858, ten years before the Parsonage was demolished.

Most residents will be familiar with the display of wildlife specimens in the museum at Prittlewell Priory put together by Christopher Parsons (1807-82). A member of the Linnæan Society, Christopher Parsons was a keen collector of birds, their eggs, butterflies, insects, and plants and, being skilled in taxidermy, he preserved most of his collection himself. Between 1825 and 1879 he collected 319 species of plants native to the district, which were summarised by Thomas M F Tamblyn-Watts and published in the *Southend Standard* in 1923. His intended work on the flora of the area was never published. For 20 years he observed and recorded local meteorological conditions. A century later, rainfall, at 20 inches a year, is much the same as it was then.

He lived at North Shoebury Hall from 1842-1870, in 1850 he was joined by marriage to Philip Benton, his wife Mary being one of Benton's elder sisters.

Those interested in local history are likely to be familiar with the name of Philip Benton (1815-98). His *History of Rochford Hundred*, written between 1867 and 1888, provides a valuable source of local information, and many of those recorded facts are used within this book. Written parish by parish it was never fully completed in his lifetime as he was overcome by paralysis. Two volumes were published in 1886-8, but it was not until 1978, when his remaining notes were discovered in an old hat box in the local records office, that the fourteen remaining parishes were written up and published by the Rochford Hundred Historical Society, an invaluable addition to local knowledge.

Philip and Sarah, his grandparents, lived in South Ockendon, where mention is made of the family in the early 17th century. Upon his marriage his father, Samuel, the youngest of five, moved to North Shoebury House to begin farming in the area. It was Samuel who rebuilt the Moated House in 1824.

Philip was born at North Shoebury House, after marriage he lived at Beauchamps, Shopland and Little Wakering Hall, he and his wife Eliza having nine children. Charlotte, his eldest daughter, married Christopher Parson's cousin, William.

When Eliza died in 1874 he married the children's governess, Elizabeth Warren, and twelve years later they moved back to North Shoebury House.

A distinguished local figure he travelled about the district in his dogcart gathering information for his notes and the lectures he gave. Like his friend, Christopher Parsons, he also donated much of his collection to the town. These were invaluable archæological finds, many brought to him by locals who knew of his interest. He died in Whitegate Road, Southend, and is buried in Shopland Cemetery. His name is still visible scratched into the brickwork of the west facing wall of North Shoebury House.

The last Lord of the Manor, Dale Knapping, was born into a local farming family. His grandfather, John, was the youngest of ten children born to Christopher Knapping who farmed at Shopland Hall before Philip Benton. John became an attorney and married Mary, the widow of John King, her maiden name, Dale, was then incorporated into the Knapping family name. He lived and farmed at Suttons and when he died left all his land and property in trust only to his male heirs.

His eldest son, Christopher Dale Knapping, farmed at South Shoebury Hall and was the father of William and Dale. William took over the farm from his father, his wife Mary was a poetess. Dale marrièd Mary Asplin, whose father farmed Wakering Hall. He became a Justice of the Peace and made a great deal of money from the brick works he established that brought employment to the local area. Caring greatly for his workers and their families he was very benevolent to the village people, providing many facilities before they were offered by the state. A great deal of his time was spent in Paris where he died in 1878 after suffering a heart attack at the Hôtel des Deux Mondes. His body was brought back for burial in St Andrew's churchyard.

Shoebury Beach

H M S *King Alfred* aground opposite the Officers' Mess, 1905

Chapter 6
INTO THE TWENTIETH CENTURY

As the people of Shoebury welcomed the new century, the population had grown to 2,990, including 988 men from the School of Gunnery. Now events and progress in the town were now inextricably linked with army activities.

One year the annual Sunday School outing was to Layzell's Farm in Blackgate Road (Elm Farm). The children were driven in a farm cart from the church, along the High Street, for a tea party and games in one of the fields. Among the games was a sweet scramble where sweets were tossed into the air for the children to scramble after, the sweets were unwrapped. Any missed were no doubt consumed by the cows when they were ushered back after the party had ended. Mr Layzell, the farmer, was nicknamed 'old Bugwhiskers' by the children because of his alarming looking full, bushy beard.

Then Blackgate Road was no more then a lane lined either side with elm trees, the black gate led into the farmland behind the manor house where an old laundry belonging to the manor had been converted to make a small farmhouse.

1901 'In the village' Shoebury Avenue, Wakering Avenue, Southchurch Avenue, Friars Street and Wallace Street were built off the High Street. 'Up the Cambridge' Trafalgar Road, Caulfield Road, Waterloo Road and Richmond Avenue were built. This year saw the advent of another public service, the fire brigade.

1902 Lord Roberts visited Shoebury to watch trials of guns against 9.2" plating. A Marconi wireless station was set up in a field just north of Love Lane Cottages in Wakering Road, it was a repeater station receiving information bounced from the Marconi station at Chelmsford. The purchase of the gas undertaking from a private company was completed, the council raising a loan of £12,306 as a part payment. The price of gas by 1906 was 5 shillings (25p) for 1,000 cubic feet.

In 1903 two steam trains were acquired by the Ministry of Defence, a six wheel-coupled locomotive named 'Shoeburyness', and a saddle-tank locomotive the 'School of Gunnery' bought from British Locomotive makers.

The *Southend Standard* of May, 1905, carried a report of the stranded H.M.S. *King Alfred*: 'Considerable excitement was created in Shoebury and Southend on Friday evening when the news sped like wildfire that the armoured cruiser *King Alfred* had run ashore on the Shoebury Sands. She had embarked with a full crew for service with the Mediterranean Squadron. She left Chatham to carry out her orders and went ashore on the Shoebury sands on Friday afternoon.

There was a moderate sea and a northeast breeze and, on receipt of the news of the mishap, the tugs *Champion* and *Primrose* put off from Sheerness to *Alfred*'s assistance. The engines were at once put full steam astern, but without effect. The tugs attempted to tow her off and their united efforts failed to move the stranded ship. More tugs were sent out from Sheerness, and about 1 o'clock on Saturday

Shoebury Beach

morning the cruiser was refloated. The sands were soft and she sustained no damage. She left the shore for the Mediterranean on Sunday. It was generally surmised that the current was changing when the mishap occurred. During Saturday many people watched the vessel from Shoeburyness and Southend Pier'.

During Shoebury Week, 1906, everyone welcomed the idea of an evening of open air theatricals on the cricket field. The troops brought forms from the barracks and the married families carried their own chairs to the event that again featured the London Company Pierrots. It was a huge success, but the next morning Gunner McKindley was dismayed to find four sackfuls of litter left behind.

1907 The first bus run from Shoebury to Southend. Requests were made this and the following year to the council as to whether work could be found for the unemployed from London. The reply was 'in the negative'.

1908 There was a fire at Wilkinson's the bike shop in the High Street opposite the chemist shop.

1909 A new Barge Pier with a steam crane was built next to Gog's Berth. Guns, ammunition and equipment were transported to the various battery locations by the government rail line. Far removed from the days when horses had to drag the equipment the four miles over unmade roads from the mainline station which then terminated in Southend. The illuminated Garrison bandstage was erected between the cricket field and the officers' tennis courts.

1910 The new council chambers (now the police station) were built in the High Street on the corner of Shoebury Avenue, at a cost of £828. Behind this the fire station was built costing £160. There was a fire at A J Harris' workshop at the end of Rampart Street.

On 13th May, 1913, the residents of Shoebury welcomed the opening of their own local cinema, the Picture Palace, seating 350 people, with a ceremonial opening and the presentation of a silver gilt key. Each year the management of the cinema would send a personal card to local children on their birthday, with two free tickets for the Saturday morning film. It was to close on 5th March, 1955, a victim of the television age. On the last night it functioned as a cinema the 'A' film, *She's back on Broadway*, with Virginia Mayo and Steve Cochrane was shown, followed by the 'B' film, *Kid Nightingale*, with Jane Wyman and John Payne. What became of the presentation key, specially made by Goodman Brothers the Southend jewellers, is not known.

Opposite, the Conservative Club opened on the corner of Seaview Road.

1915 Foulness island was purchased by the government. Opposite the railway station a Y.M.C.A. was built; this was pulled down in 1923.

On 6th April, 1916, King George V visited the New Ranges to watch a variety of equipment being fired: after lunch in the Officer's Mess he inspected the School of Gunnery. Local schoolchildren were lined up in Motts meadow, an open field between the old Friars farmhouse (then known as Motts Farm after the farmer of

Short sea plane out of fuel

A barge trip around the pier, 1906

that name) in the High Street and the Red Brick House, to see the King's entourage pass by on their way to the New Ranges. As she was so near home Hilda Cripps was allowed to go there afterwards, instead of returning to school. She remembers standing with her mother at the crossroads after her lunch hoping to catch another glimpse of the King as he was leaving. To their delight, King George, on seeing them standing alone on the dusty unmade road, raised his hat and nodded to them

Opposite Mott's field, on the other side of the High Street, was another where sunflowers were grown commercially. These lofty flowers towered far above the heads of the children and Hilda recalls one foggy evening becoming completely lost among the tall stalked flowers as she took a shortcut home.

Hilda's family lived in the row of cottages in Wakering Road just past the Red Brick House where Mr Cooper, the steward at Suttons lived, then it was known as 'Cooper's Corner'. The five pairs of cottages were built by the Knapping family and were considered to be 'ahead of their time'. Each pair had space from their adjoining neighbours and a garden at the back, each front garden was planted with a different flowering tree, an almond, japanese cherry, laburnum, or double may.

Just opposite were some black weatherboarded cottages also called the 'black huts'.

Another unexpected visitor dropped by in June this year, a Short sea plane made a forced landing on the sands when it ran out of oil.

Started as the Garrison Choir Boys Club with sixteen boys in 1902, it was officially run as the Garrison Boys Sports Club from March, 1905. Meetings were held on Tuesdays and Fridays for the sons of soldiers and ex-soldiers associated with the garrison. Board games, bagatelle, boxing gloves and cricket equipment were donated and a football team formed. At first the Garrison Theatre was used so that the boys could use the vaulting horse and the parallel bars, but when Friday night dances started in the Theatre meetings moved to the church schoolroom.

Within a year the number of boys attending had risen to 56. Gradually billiards, indoor football and cricket, water polo, tennis, table tennis and hockey were added to the list of activities, with an annual outing and a social evening becoming regular features. The socials were large affairs held in the theatre, often as many as 300 people attended with the families of the boys and officers invited.

Boy Scouts started with four patrols in 1910. During the war the club remained open for games, but no competitions until 1916, when the schoolroom was needed to billet troops. It restarted again in 1919.

THE GREAT WAR, 1914-1918
No attack was made on the garrison during the war. Aeroplanes and airships were frequently seen passing overhead as they used the Thames as their corridor on bombing raids up to London. In 1917 a bomb dropped in Wakering Road on to the onion patch of a furious Mr Waters, who lived in the black huts there, another

fell by the station and one landed on Hilly Marsh killing two horses and injuring a driver. Goody's milk shop opposite St Andrew's Church also had one fall nearby.

Shoebury became a transit camp for troops as well as remaining on active alert for any threat of invasion along the sensitive estuary. Every available space was needed and married families had to evacuate their homes to house troops on active service.

The Drill Shed once again saw service as a theatre when the Garrison Theatre was taken over as an emergency hospital in November, 1914, with 40 beds. Concert parties were given during this time by the Y.M.C.A.

When the Armistice was announced children playing in the High Street were treated to a surprise train ride to the New Ranges by the happy soldiers.

In 1919 the fleet visited Shoebury and made a fine spectacle as it anchored offshore illuminated for all to see. The Garrison Theatre reopened again in December.

ACCIDENTS

After a relatively long spell without any major accidents there were two fatal accidents in 1912 and 1913 each claiming a life.

In the first, the barrel of a gun burst and Mr Rose, an R.E. workman, died from his injuries after he was struck in the throat with a piece of wiring from the bay of number 3 gantry which was completely blown out. The second accident happened when the breechblock of an 18 pounder gun blew out killing Gunners W Pearson and H Hubbard.

Another accident in 1915 at 'K' Battery in the New Ranges resulted in the death of Captain F G Lane Poole of the Royal Military Academy when the breech flew out of a smaller gun. Five more lost their lives in 1917 when yet another breech blew out.

In total, sixteen men from the experimental department had lost their lives in mishaps while testing was taking place. But the dreadful fire that occurred at the New Ranges on 28th March, 1918, caused the whole village to be evacuated. The exodus to Southend was ordered because it was feared that damage would be as great as at Silvertown in 1917. A soup kitchen and accommodation was laid on at the Kursaal for the trail of evacuees that arrived on foot clutching their valuables after the long trek along the seafront.

The fire had started in a wooden hut when a time fuse that was being fitted to a shell was accidentally dropped. The hut was left to burn but the shells inside exploded igniting ammunition dumps nearby. These in turn sent more shells flying into the air which set fire to train wagons full of ammunition, and so it continued for twenty-four hours, explosion after explosion leapfrogging from store, to dump, to truckloads of ammunition. Although some horses lost their lives in the fire, miraculously only one person was reportedly killed, although attempts to verify this were never conclusive. This was a severe blow during a critical time of the war with £3M of essential material lost.

THE VILLAGE FIRE BRIGADE

Shoebury's first 'fire station' was opened in 1901 at the back of an off-licence in West Road. Under the Captain, Mr S Munday, were second and third officer Mr Hatcher and Mr Cause. The council provided the fire escape, hose, handcart and standpipe.

After seven years they moved to Talmage's yard in Shoebury Avenue, where the rent was 2/6d a week, and in 1910 moved to their present site in Shoebury Avenue behind the Council Chamber (now the police station).

Disharmony appears to have broken out a year later when the whole brigade resigned. It was this year that a motion had been proposed that all members of the fire brigade must be abstainers (from alcohol). The motion was lost; whether this was the cause of the resignations is not recorded but the new brigade formed manned by Mr Goodson, Mr Cook and Mr Blencowe.

Fireman H A Blencowe

Chapter 7
LIFE BETWEEN THE WARS, 1918-1939

Slowly life began to get back to normal after the war: it was a bittersweet time for many of the families living in Shoebury. Many were extremely poor, stretching meagre budgets as best they could to survive where the man of the house had returned from war to no employment.

As a child in the twenties, Grace Coppock remembers her mother supplementing the family income by taking in washing for the soldiers. Every Friday night fifty bundles would be collected and brought back home. With no washing machine or drier to rely on rainy days meant the house was festooned with washing hanging everywhere. The lines of heavy, wet material gave off steam as they dried and the damp atmosphere was very uncomfortable, but it was a necessary evil. For 1/- (5p) each bundle, containing a grey back shirt, a towel, a vest, a pair of pants and a pair of socks, was washed, mangled and ironed. The inclusion of a 'civvy' shirt earned 3d extra. The indignity of being seen wheeling the barrow load of clean bundles, tied securely in place with a rope, back to the barracks meant a devious route was followed to escape notice. This was along the alleyway behind George Street, across John Street and through Baker's Yard. Then a quick dash along the High Street and through the barrack gates to another alleyway just past the hospital, known as the 'Suez Canal'. This led directly to the billets of the 21st battery and the owners of the finished laundry.

Another means of income was providing dinners for the men working in the Model 'B' Brickfield. The basins, carefully tied in cloths, were entrusted to the children who would come home from school at mid-day to carry the dinners to the men at work. To speed up the procedure the children would 'hitch a lift' from the wagons as they trundled across the High Street, hanging on grimly with one hand as they clutched the dinner tightly in the other.

The 'rufstuf' brought in by the barges as landfill material was a great source of useful material and would be enthusiastically sorted through for anything that could be put to good use or sold. The barges also carried coal. To have picked coal from the stock piles would have been stealing, but to pick up the odd lump dropped from the barrows as the men negotiated the narrow ramps leading from the barges was nothing of the sort. 'Wobbling barrow syndrome' seems to have been a common industrial condition at the time, enabling many a local family to toast their toes and dry the washing with impunity. The fact that prams were sometimes needed to remove the coal shows the severity of the conditions suffered by the men.

Fred Cause, the Captain of the fire brigade, and his wife ran a soup kitchen. Many of the poorer families sent the children to have their jugs filled to provide a meal for the family. Others were more fortunate reaping enormous benefits from the trade generated by the garrison, and the employment it gave. A thriving parade

The Fire Brigade at Shoebury Fête, 1911
Shoebury Hotel

of shops established itself around the entrance to the barracks. Strategically placed between the Horseshoe Barracks and the New Ranges, the Old Village was a busy place with army personnel daily passing along the High Street between the two. A familiar sight on firing days was the wagons sent out to collect the spent shells, driven along the High Street usually drawn by three pairs of horses, each pair with its own rider.

The local shops thrived with so many customers: there were three butchers, two greengrocers and at least seven grocers' shops. Before bottled milk was delivered to the door the rounds were made by the local dairyman, Mr Murray, who would measure the required pint or half-pint of milk straight from the churns on his handcart into your jug or basin. When Howard's Dairies took over with deliveries of bottled milk there were two rounds a day. Bread deliveries were also made from the Co-op store and Powell's, the local baker.

Mr Clover was the first postmaster in Rampart Street, then Mr S W Coupe ran both the post office and chemist shop in Rampart Street until he moved the chemist part of the business to premises next to the barrack gate. The post office then re-opened over the road by the Shoebury Hotel, until the new one was built in George Street in 1931.

In Smith Street there were two barbers, a cobblers and a shop called Mullards which sold everything from 'a pin to a battleship', including canes, familiar in most households at the time for maintaining discipline. One person recalls that the shop opposite the station was once a small lending library, as well as selling sweets and stationery. She was forbidden by her mother to buy sweets from there as the resident cat regularly reclined in the window amongst them - in those days sweets were mainly unwrapped. Many of the early postcards feature old photographs of Shoebury taken by Mr Baker, whose wife ran the shop, and Mr Coupe.

Mr E Holmes was another local photographer with a shop in the parade that began opposite the station and along to George Street. Next to that, Jeff's Café and tearooms catered for the visitors coming up from the beach, as well as local workmen, their delicious ice cream being home made.

THE SOCIAL LIFE
In July, 1919, great efforts started to get the Theatre back in shape ready for the winter shows and months of preparation went on. An orchestra pit was cut out at the front of the stage, a box office was installed under the gallery and new scenery was made and painted. The crowning touch was the smart new lampshades made for the band by Lt Commander Maton out of 'Cerebos' salt tins. Everything was ready for the opening night on 16th December with the band now installed at the front of the stage instead of in the gallery at the back of the Theatre.

After a break of almost three years the Garrison Boys' Club restarted again with a full programme that now included in the annual programme a Fancy Dress Ball.

Girls were now permitted to join in although it still remained 'the Boys' Club'. Another addition was the yo-yo competition. Boxing was very popular with cups in five categories, midget, featherweight, lightweight, middleweight, and heavyweight. The five sons of Gunner Easton, R.A., appeared in a boxing display put on by the club at the Foulness Show, the youngest is not on record as attending the club at this time, he appears to have been a 'makeweight'.

As well as catering for the boys the garrison supplied many diversions and entertainments for the young ladies of the town, invited as they were to the regular dances and balls held in the officers' and sergeants' messes.

In 1923 two hundred cars waited in a queue ready to discharge their passengers who were guests at that evening's ball.

Shoebury Week and open days for the family restarted again in 1921.

THE PRIDE OF THE ARMY

Shoebury Gunners bring
Home the Cup

Royal Artillery (Shoeburyness 1st Batt. Royal Welsh Fusiliers (Blackdown))

On Easter Monday, at Aldershot, the Shoebury Gunners achieved their ambition by winning the Army Cup 4-0. It was the greatest win in the final for 26 years. The bands of the 2nd Batt. the North Staffordshire Regiment, and the pipes and drums of the 1st Batt. the Gordon Highlanders entertained the crowd, who thrilled to the fast pace of the match which never slowed in spite of a keen wind which blew diagonally across the pitch during the match. At half-time the score was 1-0, the goal scored by Allen in the first five minutes. The teams remained on the pitch during the interval enjoying, with the crowds the swirl of the bagpipes. Three more goals came the gunners way scored by Kemp seven minutes into the second half, then Dixey, and Kemp again. For their fine effort each member of the gunners team was presented with a gold medal by Lady May, wife of Lt. Gen. Sir Reginald May, as well as receiving the magnificent trophy they had fought so hard for, with a replica for the Royal Artillery to keep as a memento of the occasion. The runners-up each received a silver medal.

THE VILLAGE AND CAMBRIDGE TOWN DIARY

Building resumed again after the war at both ends of the town, but not on the same scale as before the war.

1920 The Mission Hall in Wakering Avenue was built, and next to St George's Roman Catholic Church a church hall was built.

1921 The old NAA building which had been put to use as the army school (hence the name School Road leading to the garrison church) was taken down by Mr Harris and re-erected opposite the station next to the shops. Opening on 14th May

The Wesleyan Sunday School, led by the Salvation Army band, marching along High Street, 1900

Troops marching to Church parade

for the use of the British Legion the opening ceremony was performed by Colonel P L Holbrooke., who also led the unveiling of the war memorial, then on the traffic island at the centre of the crossroads in front of the cinema.

Council houses were erected on the corner of Elm Road and Ness Road.

1922 77 people applied for the position of Gas Manager.

1924 Thorpedene Gardens, Tudor Gardens and Vincent Crescent, named after Councillor (Robert) Vincent Cook, were built.

Electric (battery) powered trains were introduced on the government rail line. By the following year there were eleven miles of track which now extended the five miles to Havengore Island, and to each separate firing location enabling equipment to be delivered to the exact point of use. Where the track crossed the High Street there was a small hut for the crossing keeper reached by a short flight of steps. These appeared to prove no obstacle for the gentleman concerned for, although being severely crippled, he was very adept at swinging himself up on his crutches to enter the hut.

An electricity generating station powered by an old submarine engine was set up by the old waterworks site at the Grove to supply the garrison, this was in operation until power was taken from the bulk supply in 1936.

1926 The Metropolitan Police relinquished duties at the New Ranges, replaced by the new War Department Constabulary. Rushley Island was bought for £1,000

This year the local fire brigade took delivery of a new steamer fire engine, two years later a motorized vehicle from Martin and Sons arrived. Before the arrival of these vehicles horses from the local livery stable had pulled the fire engine. The stable also provided the horses to pull the carriages for weddings and funerals, undoubtedly in many cases the same horse. Fortunately, the animals seem to have been well briefed as to that day's duties or pandemonium could have broken loose, imagine a funereal pace to attend a fire or a quick gallop to a funeral.

1927 No longer needed, the Garrison gas works were turned into gun sheds. Four store huts burnt down on Hilly Marsh; Gunner Thompson died in the fire.

1928 The Baptist Church was built at the junction of Thorpedene Gardens and Caulfield Road. Cranley Gardens and Stroma Gardens were built. The Ratepayers' Association was formed. Havengore Bridge and a concrete road to Foulness were completed after four years work.

1929 The Sunshine Home was opened by HRH Prince George in Ness Road, built on land that had once belonged to the Hall next door. Run by the Balham Hospital, it was a convalescent home for sick children from the poorer parts of London to recuperate in the healthy seaside air. In this year the Medical Officer of Health reported 'in fact it may truly be said that Shoeburyness is one of the healthiest seaside resorts in England'. Southend is renowned for its health giving ozone levels emitted from the mud at low tide. Known to chemists as O^3 the gas is a form of oxygen with three atoms in the molecule, instead of the 2 of ordinary oxygen.

The Tivoli Tea-room with the bandstand and Uncle Tom's

Shoebury Common

The Chairman of the Council, Mr W J Boosey, switched on the town's electricity supply supplied by the government generating station.

On 13th March, 1931, a fire in the barrack stables near the first Heavy Quick Firing Battery killed a number of horses, which were buried on Hilly Marsh.

Mr Oldfield opened the new Labour Club in Seaview Road, known as the Eagle Club. The new Post Office opened in George Street with Mr Read as postmaster.

A DAY AT THE SEASIDE

The depression in the thirties had brought hard times and with much unemployment in the area real efforts were now being made to try and establish the town as a holiday resort. It was hoped that new facilities would attract the visitors to Southend to 'come east'. The old Common land, measuring 8.75 acres, was designated a recreational area with amenities to encourage more visitors and in 1922 two refreshment huts were built on the Common costing £500 each. In 1925 a bandstage was erected nearby costing £200 and in 1928 Uncle Tom's Cabin was built costing £1,000.

The Cambridge end of town fared better in the attempt, offering a pleasant drive along the prom with refreshments available on arrival at the Common. The newcomers to this part of town were often retired people or commuters to London, who aspired to their genteel neighbours at Thorpe Bay, rather than those who lived in the busy, noisy, more commercial atmosphere around the barracks.

Housewives at both ends of town offered accommodation to holiday-makers who could avail themselves of beautiful walks in the surrounding countryside as well as the delights of the seashore.

At East Beach two new shelters and a tearoom were built in 1929 on the promenade at Rampart Terrace. On Wednesday evenings there was dancing to live bands there. By 1932 there were 600 deckchairs for hire.

Dale Knapping's three unmarried daughters, Margaret Helen, Edith May, and Gertrude Emma had nurtured a plan to create an exclusive, high class holiday estate along the East Beach area, but it never came to fruition. Unfortunately the cold winds that frequently blew, and the military atmosphere, complete with the regular booming of guns, was not conducive to a snooze in a deckchair. In 1933 the idea was shelved and the local newspaper covered what changes there were to be made to East Beach: 'The late Miss Knapping, Lady of the Manor of Shoeburyness, left instructions in her will that steps should be taken to beautify the Shoebury beach. To this end both the blacksmith's shop and the adjoining boat-building establishment are to come down shortly.' When Margaret Helen, the last of the Knapping sisters died in 1935 she made large bequests to the National and the Tate Galleries.

After the death of Mr Sawkins, the blacksmith, in October, 1929, his wife ran the shop with the help of a farrier until it was demolished. Mrs Sawkins continued

Sawkin's blacksmithy on the beach

Shoebury Garrison Boys' Club billiards, 1935. H Burfield and L Evans with cues

Whent's grocers on the corner of Sea View Road and West Road

Fred Simpson delivering milk to Landwick Cottages

to live in Shoebury, but died at the Metropolitan Nursing Home in Walton-on-Thames; her funeral was held on the eleventh anniversary of her husband's death.

Some well known visitors to the blacksmith's forge had been the boxers who used the gymnasium at the Shoebury Hotel for training, including Georges Carpentier, Billy Wells, J L Sullivan, Larry Gains, George Cook and Packy McFarlane. They enjoyed spending time at the blacksmith's corrugated iron and wood hut on the beach, and Carpentier, then World Heavyweight Champion, in particular enjoyed many happy hours there swinging a hammer along with the smith.

Also to come down was the boathouse. Auctioneers W J Rayner sold the timber boathouse and a quantity of tools and boat gear for £10. The 60 x 16 foot building raised only 10/-, the purchaser, Mr J Whisstock, deciding to give the timber away to any unemployed men willing to demolish it. Beach huts were installed in place of these buildings to further the image of the town as a holiday and recreational resort.

Work started on a transformer for 11,000 volts by the cinema and in June the supply was taken from the bulk supply.

On 17th May, 1933, hundreds of people thronged the road and railway bridge in Elm Road to see the opening of the new playing field. The Lord-Lieutenant of Essex, General R B Colvin, and his wife, Lady Gwendoline, performed the opening ceremony. Shoebury Urban District Council raised a loan of £790 to fund this 6¾ acre amenity, with facilities for football, cricket, tennis and bowls. The bandstage from the common was moved to the new park and erected just inside the entrance, Councillor F Desborough gave the water fountain in memory of his late wife.

In July the bridge in Elm Road was reconstructed and widened.

Mrs Allen recalls the travelling fair that came every year around the end of the 'twenties and early 'thirties. to camp on the waste ground where Bridge Garage is now or in a field along Elm Road. Gypsies came as well selling their goods. A Jewish gentleman living at Bridge House would bring stockings home from the Petticoat Lane market to sell. The young girls would go to the house to buy them and she remembers the surprise she had as they waited at the door to see that his tablecloth was always a newspaper spread on the table.

On 1st October, 1933, Shoebury became part of the County Borough of Southend and R Vincent Cook, Fred Cause and Albert Farrow were elected to represent the ward.

Under Inspector Christie and Sergeant Cheadle, eight constables from the Southend Police department now took over policing responsibilities for Shoebury. Within a year a new police box graced the High Street near the station and work began on a new police station and quarters in Elm Road.

The new Rectory, built in 1868 to replace the old parsonage at the Grove, was on open land off Church Road near where Raven Farmhouse and Gardens had once stood. It was set back and secluded, approached by a winding driveway. There was an orchard where Waterford Road is today, the gardener was Mr Turner. Mrs Allen tells me her sister was the maid there. A spring ran under the house, home to several families of rats. She recalls that one day the Reverend Ellis Jones persuaded her sister to accompany him there and hold aloft a hurricane lamp so enabling him to see sufficiently to shoot the rats. From the basement a large back staircase ran up to the old attics. This rectory was pulled down in 1934 when the land was sold to Burges Estates and the new one, still in use today, was built beside the church on the site of the old mortuary, in its turn demolished to accommodate the new building.

Later that year, a new Children's Home run by Southend Council was built on the land where the old rectory had stood. Called 'Seaview' the homes were built to replace 'The Grange' in Southend, on the corner of Southchurch Road and Southchurch Avenue. The first matron was Miss Thompson.

There were five houses, Merrytrees, Woodlands, St Christopher, Amethyst, and Oak, each housing ten children aged between three and eighteen years. Three of the houses had housemothers the other two were run by married couples, with the husband following his own occupation.

In 1974 care was transferred to Essex County Council when they took responsibility for Social Services from the council. During the war Richmond Avenue School was used to billet troops and the children who were not evacuated were given their lessons at the Seaview Homes where each house had the advantage of its own air raid shelter. In the early eighties, as less accommodation was needed, the Homes closed and the children were transferred to a smaller establishment in Avenue Road, Westcliff.

Today, the cul de sacs Knollcroft and Noredale occupy the land. The open land behind (now Leitrim Avenue) was once used as the recreational ground for the Starline Paint Company, of Grainger Road, Southend.

Also in 1934 the houses opposite the post office in George Street were built, on the edge of the old East Beach brickfield.

On the 11th February, 1936, people awoke to find the sea along the shoreline frozen over by a band of ice 100 yards wide. The shallow water left behind when the tide had receded in the early hours of the morning had frozen. The returning tide lifted this layer, floating it on the surface until the tide receded once more thinning the ice out over a larger area. This thin layer gradually thickened to a depth of six inches, effectively acting as a barrier blocking off the next incoming tide, which simply seeped underneath, freezing and adding to the depth of ice. When the tide receded once more icebergs a foot thick were left stranded on the shore.

FOLLOWING OUR LANDMARKS

After 1925 Crouchman's farm was leased by the Kelmsley family to tenants.

Burges Estates, a company set up by Major Burges, now owned the South Shoebury Hall and all the common land to the south. In 1929 a strip of this land was sold to build the Sunshine Convalescent Home. The Hall and the remaining twenty acres of land were leased to Captain H I R Townend, R.N., and his wife on a 21 year lease, then it was planned the house would be demolished due to the poor condition of the property. They put the common land to use for breeding musk-rats, a project that was short-lived after the government intervened, so they turned instead to poultry farming.

At the Hall Mrs Townend bred cocker spaniels and offered farmhouse teas, which were served on the lawn adjacent to the new convalescent home. Quite unexpectedly a new business developed from people arriving at the house requesting permission to set up their tents on the land by the hen runs. This proved to be a more lucrative venture than all the others, so now the land stretching from the convalescent home to Shore House was used purely as a tented camping site run by the couple. It was very popular with people from London, who would arrive at the station and catch a bus 'up to the Cambridge' for a penny.

In those days the Hall provided straw, obtained from Gallagher's Farm, Wakering, for the palliasses. One local lad recalls that just before the war he earned the princely sum one weekend of 3/6d for trundling barrow loads of new straw to the site and returning with the used straw to be burned.

When war broke out in 1939, Captain Townend once more enlisted in the navy, the third war in which he would see service.

Mr Prentice ran a fleet of six buses in competition with the Westcliff Bus Company, who later bought him out. The buses parked on a piece of land south of Dangers Bridge. An enormous scrap yard owned by Mr Cooper, who lived at Moat House, was also on this land. The pile of scrap, much of it ex-army, was piled so precariously high it often toppled over on to the road. This was known as Chick's Dump until it was demolished after the war and bungalows were built on the land.

Farming was no longer the mainstay of the area, but continued in North Shoebury. Barley replaced rye, with corn, potatoes and beans as the main crops.

On 23rd May, 1934, a reporter from the *Daily Sketch* was despatched to Wakering hot-foot for a story after rumours of discontent had spread. Under the headline:

> IT'S NOT THE GREAT GUN THEY FEAR
> BUT THERE IS A GRIEVANCE
>
> ------ - ------- - --#--- - ------ - -----------
>
> Great Wakering Folk Do Not Like Those Red
> Flags of the War Department
>
> -

Their special correspondent reported he came down here today to look at a neighbour-hood said to be in a state 'approaching fear' over the expected trials in the vicinity of a new giant gun bigger than the residents have ever seen or heard. A long day's search both in Great Wakering itself and Shoeburyness revealed no sign of panic. 'I did find however deep seated in many people a sense of grievance against the War Department'.

It seemed that most people interviewed accepted the presence of the guns and the noise believing the area to be the one place in the country where the trials could be carried out. But they resented greatly the feeling that the government was riding over them roughshod, eroding their public rights.

'A much more objectionable feature of the landscape is the red flag danger signal, which flies with aggravating persistency warning people off their neighbouring hard sands.' In spite of only one gun being fired that afternoon some distance away the gates and flags at the beginning of the Broomway were preventing access.

Residents complaints ranged from difficulty in getting compensation for windows broken by the blasts; excessive, unnecessary closures of roads to the beach when firing is not occurring, 'awaiting proper conditions' the authorities claimed; when red flags were flying fishermen could not go back and retrieve the lines they had set earlier, thus their catches benefited the birds rather than their dinner table.

Not everyone shared the same opinion and found no hindrance and claimed a day pass would allow you to venture to Foulness. Mr Sam Carter, landlord of the Shoebury Hotel, summed up most people's feelings that they had adapted to the sound of gun testing. He felt the guns from the Isle of Grain across the estuary could be heard as clearly. Any dropping off of visitors he attributed to 'hard times' rather than the 'fresh dread of a new gun'.

It seems that curiosity rather than awe or fear was their reaction to the months of preparation observed for the new gun soon expected to arrive and believed to be destined for the defence of Singapore.

16.25 inch gun (110 tons) and 6 Pr Hotchkiss

Chapter 8
WORLD WAR II, 1939-1945

The rôle of Shoebury Garrison was mainly as a transit camp for personnel during the war, extra accommodation was urgently needed to house the thousands of troops who passed through. Huts were erected on the cricket field, and the gymnasium in Campfield Road was put into operation as a billet for troops of the 5th Maritime Regiment, others being billeted in private houses around the town. The maritime units provided artillery protection for the defence of merchant shipping.

Those children from Richmond Avenue School who were not evacuated were transferred elsewhere for their lessons, some to the children's home in Ulster Avenue, others to the Secondary School in Caulfield Road which was also being used as a Civil Defence post and housed a hospital ward, thus enabling the school buildings in Richmond Avenue to be used as extra accommodation for the army. One of the buildings became a cookhouse and those billeted in nearby houses would go there for their food, behind the houses on the south side of the school air raid shelters were erected on the field.

During the war years Shoeburyness, along with Sheerness on the opposite bank, once again became the sentinels of the river, guarding the approaches to London from 'E' boat attack, warning of approaching enemy aircraft and, where possible, stopping their progress.

The government took over Shore House in 1939 for use as a lookout post to observe the entrance to the Thames. That building was pulled down in 1946.

A series of defensive strategies were used to impede the progress of the enemy whose main target was the capital and docks upriver. Visible today the most obvious reminder of those days is the boom stretching out from East Beach. The original boom was constructed from Oregon pine and concrete, but this was replaced in 1950 with a construction of concrete uprights instead of wood. An identical fixture extended out from the Kent coastline at Sheerness, these effectively reduced the entrance of the Thames to a narrower, and more manageable shipping lane. This could be closed off completely with submarine nets blocking enemy E-Boats from sliding into the river undetected.

Many of the secrets of ship-laid magnetic mines had been solved when two were washed up on the sands, but now the new problem of mines dropped from aircraft by parachute had to be addressed. When one was discovered lying just off the beach the services of the nearest press photographer were enlisted. He was sworn to secrecy and obliged to hand over the film before it was developed. Through the night, after hurried work, a set of rough brass tools were produced and the attempt next day to diffuse the bomb was recorded by dictating to someone sitting a safe distance away. It was a finely balanced race against the incoming tide and possibe disaster if the bomb exploded. The parachute was discovered some way off.

Maunsell Army Forts after the ladders and walkways had been dismantled to deter squatters

The boom

Beyond the boom the remnants of another of the Estuary's defence systems, the sea forts, can still be seen. Named after their designer, Guy Maunsell, the function of these manned forts was to attack approaching formations of enemy aircraft on bombing raids and mine laying missions and protect the vital sea-lanes to London and the east coast ports. The forts were equipped with Bofors 40 mm guns and 3.7" heavy anti-aircraft guns. Mounted searchlights pinpointed the targets, which later in the war included flying bombs fired from Holland. Radar systems gave early warning of attack from air and sea, which was relayed to shore defences by telephone links, from where it could be quickly passed to possibly threatened areas or to vulnerable shipping.

As oil-rigs today are constructed elsewhere and then towed into position, so were the forts. Constructed by Holloway Bros. in 1942/43 at the Red Lion Wharf, Northfleet, they were built mainly of reinforced concrete because of the wartime steel shortage. They were so robust that they survived twenty-five years without maintenance.

Four forts were established in the estuary, three were army forts, one was naval.

The three Army Forts were

	U5	Nore Sands	5 miles off Sheerness
('U' for Uncle')	U6	Red Sands	7 miles off Ramsgate
	U7	Shivering Sands	8 miles off Herne Bay

The forts were composed of seven independent towers positioned 100 feet apart and connected by steel walkways. Each tower, 90 feet high and weighing 750 tons, carried a three storey steel house. Spread between the seven towers were the men's quarters and ancillary services necessary to maintain their operation, the guns were mounted above. After the war they no were no longer required for defence.

The Nore Sands Fort was dismantled in 1959/60 after being hit twice by shipping. The first collision was in March, 1953, when the Swedish pulp carrier *Baalbeck* ran into the G4 Bofors Tower, resulting in the deaths of four civilians. A year later a second ship, the *Mairola*, collided with it.

The Shivering Sands Fort suffered a similar incident in June, 1963, when its G4 tower was hit by the *Ribersborg*. Further indignities were to follow when pirate radio stations were in vogue: Screaming Lord David Sutch broadcast his 'Radio Sutch' station from the fort during the summer of 1964. This subsequently became Radio City when Reg Calvert took over the airwaves. He was killed during an 'inter-pirate disagreement' and his wife then ran the station it until its demise.

The Red Sands Fort was home between 1964 and 1967 to the pirate Radio Stations Radio Invicta, Radio King and Radio 390, who all broadcast from it. The Offshore Broadcast Act, 1967, silenced all the offshore pirate radio stations and the forts were abandoned. To prevent squatters gaining further access the Admiralty removed the ladders and walkways.

The Naval Fort HMF *Tongue Sand* was not visible from Shoebury. Weighing 4,500 tons its construction and appearance was completely different to the Army design. Sited on a pontoon were two hollow, cylindrical towers, both base and towers were constructed of reinforced concrete. The columns housed seven decks; the lower two for stores and ammunition, the top one contained the generators, the four decks in between were crew's quarters. The columns supported a platform carrying a steel superstructure of four decks. The 'bridge' housed the galley, office, and officers' quarters, above were the sea-water and fresh water tanks and the control room surmounted by the radar equipment. Tongue Sand Fort sank during a storm in February, 1996.

Sixty-seven men died when the tanker *Arinia* was mined off Shoeburyness in 1941.

From Shoebury Common (West Beach) the dark hulk of the *Phoenix* wreck, protruding from the sea looking like the hull of an overturned boat, can be seen in the distance towards Southend. This was one of the floating, concrete 'Spud Piers', for the floating Mulberry Harbour that were assembled as docking platforms for the ships and troops landing on the beaches of Normandy during the D-Day operation in 1944. Many sections were made up-river at Barking where large pits were cut in the soft mud banks of creeks and inlets to act as moulds for the concrete piers. This one was being brought down from the Humber when it developed problems and was 'parked' in the estuary, but one hundred and thirty-five exited across the Channel *en route* to Arromanches.

Two hundred and three ships, protected from enemy infiltration amongst their lines by the barrier of the boom, waited between Shoebury and Southend for the signal that the invasion was to begin. On 6th June, 1944, under cover of darkness the order came to leave the estuary, beyond the protective arms of the booms, and over to France.

The task of keeping the fighting forces supplied with ammunition, fuel and stores meant a steady stream of vessels leaving and entering the Thames. The American Liberty Ship the *Richard Montgomery* was one of these. It too ran aground and broke its back in the estuary - though nearer to Sheerness. The masts can still be seen protruding above the water from Southend. Some of the cargo was removed in August, 1944, but because it contains three thousand tons of explosives it still has to undergo regular safety checks.

The Nore sand bank, 5 nautical miles east of Southend Pier marks the entrance to the estuary.

To disable the armaments at Shoebury the Germans bombed the New Ranges in 1940. On one day alone, 18th August, 300 tons of bombs were dropped.

One gentleman, standing outside the air raid shelter in his West Road garden, got a nasty surprise as he stood watching one raid in progress. In all, five bombs were dropped; one at Friars Street, another nearby at the railway footbridge, one on WD property, and one that failed to explode on the telephone exchange. He had a grand-stand view of the fifth, which sadly scored a direct hit and killed him. Mr Moorhouse, the owner of the Kursaal who lived in Shoebury Cottage on the seafront, off Church Road, was a little luckier, only his home was hit.

Three months later one resident recalls another bombing raid. As a boy he was cycling with a friend near the coastguard station on the common when the alert sounded and a group of twelve planes, Italian Fiat VR 20s and CR 42s flying in a box formation, approached along the estuary. Taken in by the coastguard, the boys watched as guns on the beach, assisted by the mobile gun brought down from St Augustine's in Thorpe Bay and those on the pier, opened fire and brought down eleven of the planes. The remaining one dropped his bombs and headed as fast as possible back home.

Any foreign aircrew killed locally were interred in St Andrew's churchyard, in a corner by the rectory. After the war their bodies were exhumed and repatriated to their own countries or to the large German war cemetery at Cannock Chase. This was later sold to the German government for a nominal sum so that it could be classed as German soil.

To foil any invasion attempts from the sea East Beach was mined and the public was prevented from entering the area by long coils of barbed wire that stretched along the shore. Unfortunately one boy, ignoring the danger, crawled underneath the barrier, triggering a mine which exploded causing him to lose a leg. A soldier alerted by the blast hurried to his assistance and was killed instantly by another mine.

Mrs Churchill paid a visit to Shoebury during the '40s and opened a centre for the women of the Auxiliary Territorial Service (A.T.S.) in Wakering Road, just north of the military police quarters, now Chestnut Cottages. It provided a quiet haven away from the male environment of the barracks.

The official opening over, she chatted to the girls and found them most appreciative of the new laundry facilities provided for them, a welcome bonus in times of shortages and rationing. She confided that 'Winston' would wear a shirt for only a matter of hours and then change it for a new one. The amount of laundry generated was becoming a matter of concern in such austere times and so she had said to her housekeeper, 'Nellie, we must do something about this. The shirts aren't dirty just iron them and hang them up again'. But Winston had rumbled the plan and thundered, 'Woman, I will do almost anything for my King and Country, but 'hotted up shirts', never!'

Collection points were set up for collecting metal for the war effort, Hilda Cripps says her back garden looked like 'Steptoe's' yard with saucepans and other household goods destined for the armaments factories.

Although Shoebury was deemed a possible target for enemy bombs the farming village of nearby Great Wakering was not considered to be at risk and the people there were not evacuated. But after the fall of France in 1940, and the evacuation of Dunkirk, fears grew of a possible German invasion at any point along the coast.

Hilda tells of 'invasion committees' being formed under a very strict veil of secrecy, covering an area 20 miles inland from the Wash around to Rye, in Sussex. A visit from the garrison commandant in June that year requested the assistance of such a committee in Wakering to keep essential services going and to keep up local morale in any such an event. Iron rations were to be prepared and stored in readiness in secret locations, and local wells were tested for an alternative supply of suitable drinking water if needed. In the Congregational church hall in the High Street a stock of 420 papier-mâché coffins was stored, and strict instructions were given that should any fighting take place in the area the roads were to be kept free for army use. Within three months, after the Battle of Britain, the fear of invasion receded.

1945 GARRISON VICTORY SHOW (compiled from a report in a local paper).

Whitsun this year saw a wonderful show put on by the army in grateful thanks to the people of Southend and the surrounding district for their kindness and hospitality shown to the troops during the war. Unlike other parts of England where it was rainy, Shoebury saw some sunshine for the three day event, albeit a little chilly. Many of the weapons displayed had just come off the secret list, and for one shilling (5p) folks could fire a tracer bullet at targets out at sea. It was a happy day for one 83 year old, Mr Aspin, who was revisiting the garrison where he had served sixty-one years previously in the Royal Horse Artillery.

The attractions included a funfair, miniature railway, pony rides and a children's playground. The sideshows were packed and the prizes more than a little novel; five people, including two from Shoebury High Street, Mr Church and Mr Gadbolt, won live pigs. Quite relieved was Mrs Williams from Thorpe Bay, who won a bicycle.

After dusk, dances were held in the gymnasium, dancing to the 5th Maritime Melody Makers, and in the Garrison Theatre to the Royal Artillery Band. The dances ended at midnight. There were gymkhana displays, various sporting events and a cricket match, army displays of many sorts and judging competitions. One horse was injured and had to be put down after colliding with a limber during a demonstration of gun carriage manoeuvres. The 56 horses whose job it was to work on the ranges hauling guns and ammunition were on display in the stables being attended by their grooms, and barrack rooms were open to be peeped into.

In the exhibition enclosure there were displays of weapons. Ten Ton Tessie, Block-Buster and Tirpitz-Buster, three 1200 lb R.A.F. bombs stood towering upwards like the pillars at Stonehenge. A Naval or coast gun capable of hurling a one ton shell over the Straits of Dover, and an assortment of other war hardware created a great deal of interest.

On Sunday the Drumhead Service reminded everyone of the more serious side of war. Members of the Royal Artillery Association had been met at the station by detachments of gunners and ATS and escorted to the ground by the Royal Artillery Band where the choir of the Garrison Church had assembled.

After the service, led by the Rev Naylor, DSO, MBE, ME, Senior Chaplain to the Essex Area, the 250 members of the RAA wearing their last war medals joined the other participants in the quarter mile column that marched past General Cunningham, who took the salute. Afterwards they enjoyed a reunion in the theatre.

VE-day street parties. The lower picture is Caulfield Road, looking east towards Ness Road

Three badges closely associated with the Garrison - the Royal Army Chaplains' Department, the Royal Engineers and the Royal Artillery

Chapter 9
AFTER THE WAR

Shoebury prepared to settle down after the war. There was still the feel of a small country community separated from the neighbouring villages by open countryside. Both Church Road and Caulfield Road petered out into the fields that separated Shoebury from Thorpe Bay, and north of Caulfield Road and Elm Road was farmland.

It was quite an adventure as a child to head down the tree-lined lane beside the water tower in Elm Road to the pond at 'Bunkers', by the new Friars Farm. This pond was one of the three pits dug out by Mr Millbank during the thirties depression when farming alone could not support the family. Sand was dug out and supplied to the building trade as far away as Southend and Leigh to supplement his income. Another of these pits filled in with landfill was not considered suitable for building land and so became the sports field in Elm Road.

My own recollections of this time are attending St Peter's Sunday School in the High Street, run by Miss Ruegg and Miss Cannon. Once a month the Sunday School children joined the church service at St Peter's in Hinguar Street. In 1947 I started at Richmond Avenue School. Meet anyone who went to Richmond Avenue School in the 40s and 50s and they will undoubtedly remember Miss Davey. She was an enigma in the post war greyness, this very short, very round, very feisty, very blonde lady with very short hair, of a very indeterminate age wearing very bright makeup. She was just so 'very'. I can remember her asking our class of 9 year old girls and boys whether they thought she was wearing stockings or (the very 'new' and very fashionable) nylons? I can't remember which now, or the significance of the question. Mr Poutney, Mr Read, Mr Hudson, Mr Phillips, Miss Cody, and Miss Fortescue were all there too.

1953 was the coronation year of Queen Elizabeth II and, in common with others all over the country, street parties were held to celebrate the event. Southend Council gave each child a souvenir cup, saucer and plate.

But celebrations had not been the order of the day at the beginning of the year. By comparison to their neighbours to the north and west, the residents of Shoebury escaped lightly in the dreadful floods of February, 1953. The island of Foulness was cut off for two days. At Landwick and Great Wakering people were evacuated from their homes after retreating to upper floors and being trapped until rescue arrived. In Southend the depth of the water reached eight and a half feet in Peter Pan's Play-ground, the height of the water is still shown on the outside wall of the Crooked House.

The New Ranges were the most badly affected part of Shoebury itself. Men from the garrison fought tirelessly, often from dawn to dusk, over the following three weeks to help the civilian population of the surroundings. Using the dual purpose, boat shaped wagons, known as DUKWs, that could travel as well in water as on dry land, they struggled to rescue stranded people, animals, property and belongings in cold, wet and miserable conditions and repairing and restoring order from the chaos left behind when the waters receded. Many animals were drowned, hen houses sailed away with their occupants and fortunate creatures were seen floating by on pieces of timber. The garrison provided hot tea to newly rescued folk before they were redirected, and supplied 400 blankets to one local parish council.

It had started on Saturday, 31st January, when high winds during the day, reaching Force 6 (strong), and heavy gusts sent huge waves crashing on to the shore. Southend lifeboat was launched three times. When the lunchtime tide receded it did not drop back as far as usual, prevented from doing so by the strong winds blowing on shore, which compounded the problems to come.

That night, as the next high tide approached, the alarm was raised by the on-duty military policeman at Taylor's Hut at the junction of Foulness and Havengore Island. He reported by phone around 11 pm, to the War Department Headquarters at Blackgate Road, that water was lying two feet deep on Havengore Island and he needed to warn the local stockman because his sheep were dashing around in fright. Two huge surges of water, several feet high, swept in from two directions engulfing the land and drowning the policeman who had raised the alarm as he tried to climb on to the flat roof of the two storey building he occupied.

With an hour still left to high tide the water was already at the top of the sea walls, when finally it swept over the top it flooded into the Old Ranges. Then, tearing down a 180 yard stretch of the sea defences in the New Ranges, it raced north to the already stricken Foulness and Havengore Islands, south to Blackgate Road, and west at Morrins Point in the ranges towards Great Wakering. At midnight the mean wind speed at Shoebury rose from fresh to strong (22 to 27 mph), persisting for three hours with intermittent gusting, at 1.10 am one gust reached 56 mph.

The high winds continued the next day until the afternoon. Rescue links were hampered because the railway lines between Benfleet and Leigh were flooded, trapping many of the trains so badly needed to transport people away from the stricken area at the rail depot at Shoeburyness. These were able to proceed slowly through by 3rd February to provide a Benfleet to London service, but through services from Shoebury to London in both directions were not established for another six days.

The Sunshine Home at Shoebury was without gas for cooking or most of its heating. Once the fire brigade had cleared the pumping station in Ness Road, late in the evening of 2nd February, it was possible to reduce the water level on Shoebury Common. The swollen River Shoe overflowed and claimed the lives of some unsuspecting cats behind the cinema; it is rumoured that elsewhere a local pig met with a similar fate.

It had been a textbook scenario. After the floods of January, 1928, the Liverpool Observation and Tidal Institute had made a detailed study of North Sea storm surges, based on tidal information taken from observations at Southend. It found that these surges were caused by the drag of the wind across the surface of the sea drawing up volume of water and then setting in motion as a separate surge, quite independent of the tide. The strength and duration of the wind influences the volume of water raised, as does the wind direction. When the surge coincides with a high tide, especially the very high Spring Tides, it can be disastrous.

***

Over the years the narrow ribbon of land sandwiched between the railway line and Campfield Road, stretching from the Grove to Smith Street, had housed temporary or overflow residents of the garrison when extra space was needed.

Firstly this had been the tented accommodation from whence the road derived its name, and during WWII huts had been erected there, as well as on Hilly Marsh, to house troops brought in on active service. By the 1950s, it was the young men doing their National Service who found it their home for the two years of their compulsory service. None was there by choice, many came from small towns and villages in the north and found the 'southerners' aloof and unfriendly. Shoeburyness, whose railway sidings appeared larger than the town itself, was not where they wanted to be.

The billets and cookhouse were on the site of Amstrad, next to the 'Birdcage Quarters'. There was a parade ground for 'square bashing', and a small building just beyond the level crossing gate housed the tailors who sewed on their badges and emblems. The gymnasium was used as such and also served as a dance hall for occasional dances.

One of the regiments to serve at the garrison during this period was the 36th Guided Weapon Regiment, R.A., the first to be armed with a British manufactured guided weapon, the English Electric 'Thunderbird'. They were welcomed in the spring of 1959, unfortunately without their missiles for a while. When this strip of land was sold off in the 70s it was developed as the factory site we see today.

During the early fifties a spate of arson attacks occurred in the garrison and a soldier was eventually charged with the offenses. First the old theatre, still being used as the YMCA (a rôle it adopted during the war), was burned down in 1954. Play rehearsals, which usually took place on the stage behind the curtains, were going on that evening, while the main hall was in use for other activities like bingo or card games. The church hall was also destroyed by fire, and another was set in the stables.

Made by craftsmen at the New Range workshops the Garrison had new gates installed at the Main (East) Gate and West Gate entrances.

During the 50s, under the ownership of John Ford, Crouchman's was renamed the Lansdowne Country Club. Late night drinking until the small hours prompted a police raid on the premises in November, 1953. On forcing an entry nineteen officers found not only illegal drinking after hours, but two of the rooms upstairs being used for immoral purposes. The club lost its licence and was not allowed to operate for a year. When it was sold in 1956 the new owner used the land to market sea moss and started a small holiday caravan park.

THE TOWN

Shoebury had changed little in appearance from before the war. Since the thirties, when the depression and a reduction in the number of troops present had meant economic cutbacks, very little building had happened in the town. Armagh, Antrim, Ulster, Leitrim and Waterford Roads had gradually been added over the years, also Elm and Bridge Close. The MoD houses in Blackgate and Peel Road were built on the orchard of 'old Bugwhisker's' Elm Farm. Behind the houses in the High Street were allotments (now Gunners Road), and beyond them the government single rail line ran to the ranges. The disused and overgrown marm banks running parallel with this on the beach side were almost a civic amenity, enjoyed as they were by dog walkers, courting couples and youngsters. The raised, banked sides of each shallow, square shaped hollow that had once retained the marm, had been left standing in a row, the old 'ten range'.

Overgrown with trees and bushes they made a fine adventure playground and meeting place for teenagers. One tall tree curved over the side of a pit and a thick steel hawser had been suspended from the topmost branches; knotted at one end it looked rather like a conker on a string. The brave and foolhardy climbed the tree to balance precariously on a small protuberance on the trunk where they would wait to catch the hawser as it was swung up towards them, jumping out into the abyss hoping to negotiate and sit on the knot whilst airborne. Alighting was no less a challenge, choosing the right moment to jump off on to the raised bank, failure to do so meant dangling like a fish on a rod waiting to be helped down. Although padded with material the steel threads still prickled the seat, and on one occasion claimed the seat of my trousers. The old marm banks were finally levelled and became a caravan site.

North Shoebury still had only seven people on the electoral roll, including the two Miss Mays from the Pyghtle. On election days two council officers and the local policeman would sit and wait in the small, corrugated iron village hall next to St Mary's pond that served as the polling station until all seven had been to cast their votes. For local elections this could mean a wait from 8 am until 9 pm, general elections could mean even a longer day, 7 am to 10 pm.

BUILDING BEGINS AGAIN

Development began again on the extreme western border of the town around the mid-50s. Church Road was extended and Bunters Avenue and Blyth Avenue built

Rampart Street, E M Potton's grocery ('Little Parkins': 'Big Parkins' was in High Street); Jackson's sweet shop next door.

High Street, Chapman's grocery

at the end of Caulfield Road. Shoebury and Thorpe Bay were finally seamed together by Maplin Way. The line of this road followed the old tramway that had carried thousands of bricks down to the beach for carriage from the Milton Hall brickfields north of the railway line, land that had at once been the farmlands of Samuel's Farm.

Next, the land between Caulfield Road and the railway line was filled in with the Delaware Housing Estate. A new residential home for the elderly and Thorpedene Junior School were included in the plans to cater for the needs of both ends of the new residents' age groups. A lending library was built by Maplin Bridge to replace that housed in a small shop in Ness Road, opposite Grove Road.

The estate was built on the fields that had once been Cook's Farm many years ago. The farmhouse at the junction of Ness Road and Elm Road was pulled down in 1906. For many years before building began the land had been used as allotments, some people even had sties and kept their own pigs.

The Cooks were an old Shoebury family, who built the large house called Brickeen on Mott's field in the High Street. Three of the brothers, George, Sid and Alf ran the butcher's shop in the High Street, on the corner of George Street. Harold was involved in the brick making industry.

The open space behind the Palace Cinema was once Cook's sandpit. Sand had been removed over the years for the building industry and it resembled a small quarry. At one time the land must have been raised there as, using the open space as a short cut to the playing fields in Elm Road, the grassy edge of the dug out area resembled a small cliff, sloping upwards to a stile at the crown of the bridge. It was the site used to hold the visiting fairs that came to Shoebury each year. Now the Towerfield factory site occupies the area.

Next to Brickeen the Goslings were built on the tennis courts that belonged to the old Friars Farmhouse, for many years the home of the House family. Mrs House arranged concert parties or a pantomime every year in St Peter's Hall with local children taking part.

In 1963 two areas in Shoebury were designated be upgraded as part of the Southend Borough's redevelopment schemes in the town although it was several years before these schemes were to come to fruition, and then Hinguar Street was not included as planned.

In 1972 the Department of the Environment advised the people in Rampart Street and John Street that 39 houses were to be pulled down and replaced by flats for older residents. Incensed at the implication that their homes were substandard the people who lived there requested an inquiry, but it was unsuccessful in preventing the planned demolition. Compensation was awarded according to the standard of maintenance of each property. Residents were housed temporarily in new homes off Elm Road and were given the chance of returning to live in the new flats when they were completed.

It was during the 70s that the Towerfield and Vanguard Way factory estates were built to provide work for the new influx of people already coming into the area. Even greater plans were afoot, destined, it was envisaged, to bring many more people, services and jobs to Shoebury.

Attention was focused on the Maplin Sands area once again, with feasibility studies being undertaken as to the possibility of building the third London Airport off the coast. The original plan, the dream-child of consulting engineer Bernard Clark, was announced in the *Daily Telegraph* in June, 1967, and the Roskill Commission was set up to investigate the four sites under consideration, the others being Cublington in Buckinghamshire, Nuthamstead in Hertfordshire and Thurleigh in Bedfordshire. Each site had its own vociferous band of environmental objectors, the local campaign against the airport being built off the Shoebury coast being led by Derrick Wood.

The main stumbling block at Foulness and Shoebury was the secret nature of the work on the island, and the MoD firing range and the cost of relocating it elsewhere, a difficult task in itself because there seemed little in the way of suitable alternative sites. Naturalists feared for the habitat of the Brent Black geese and the effect on their visits to the area. The great flocks of these birds could have posed the danger of 'bird strikes' to planes. Fog over the marshy land was another minus to be considered.

The plan to bring the new airport to Maplin was backed by two consortiums. TAG, the Thames Aeroport Group, made up of private companies, and TEDCO, Thames Estuary Development Company, which included the Port of London Authority, Essex County Council and Southend Borough Council.

Parliament passed a special law extending the jurisdiction of the PLA to include Maplin Sands. Plans were also drawn up for a massive deep water dock and an oil terminal in the vicinity. There was great excitement at the prospect of thousands of new jobs and a new town of half a million people was envisaged to house the workforce.

Southend Corporation invested £100,000 in promoting the area and TEDCO began talks with British Rail on the possible introduction of a new rail link between the proposed airport and King's Cross Station in London. The new spur line was to branch off the main line at Maplin Bridge and cut diagonally north east across open farmland, passing between New Farm and Moat House, to just south of Poynter's Lane. Here it would continue eastward through MoD land to the coast north of Wakering Stairs. Another proposal put forward was for a monorail link, a journey of 46 miles taking just 20 minutes to make the connection to London.

Meanwhile, Bernard Clark was nurturing his dream out on the sands. There were many consultations with Dutch specialists in land reclamation. The proposal was for a 14 square mile, man-made, island out in the estuary to house the infrastructure. The surrounding shallow water would act as a dampening system in the event of an aircraft ditching on takeoff or landing, the most critical point of any air journey, and the soft sands would cushion the impact. Experiments with the stabilisation of the sands were carried out and as a result Shoebury inherited a large hump of sandbank, still clearly visible beyond the boom. It inherited little else, the excitement of the much talked about new fast rail link with London died along with the other dreams that such a scheme would bring to the area.

In spite of an announcement in the Commons on 26th April, 1971, by John Davies, Secretary of State for Trade and Industry, that Foulness was to become the Third London Airport at an estimated cost of £500 million pounds, it never materialised. No mammoth dock or oil terminal were built, no high speed rail link either. Shoebury Station looks much the same as it did when it first opened in 1884, except that electric trains have replaced steam.

The 200 metre long 'island' left as a legacy is to now be protected as a bird sanctuary, part of the Southend-on-Sea Foreshore Nature Reserve, particularly for several varieties of tern who are present during the spring and summer months in large numbers. Work is being undertaken to combat what erosion has taken place and to raise the height of the island by one metre by gathering and replacing the surrounding displaced sand.

North Shoebury Hall, having stood empty for two years while consideration was being given to refurbish it, burnt down beyond repair in 1968.

Roy Millbank, who had been born at the newer Friars Farmhouse, now worked North Shoebury Farm. During the 1960s local market gardening began to decline: it was labour intensive and, as demand slackened as the supermarkets imported salad and vegetables, Mr Millbank reverted to farming cereal crops. He continued farming barley until his lease ran out, when the site of the Hall and the farm were sold for development. The owners, Southend-on-Sea Estates, formed by Thomas Dowsett, first Mayor of Southend, owned most of the land at North Shoebury.

Since 1930 Hall Farm Caravan Site on South Shoebury Hall Farm had become very popular, especially as a rural retreat for people from London who enjoyed a break from the city. Before the war a few caravans had gradually started to appear and after the war the number increased steadily. At first visitors came mainly for weekend visits but many, as they retired, began spending whole summers there, bringing their televisions and pets with them, regarding it almost as a second home.

In 1950 the original lease of the Hall and land was extended until 1974, then the Hall was purchased by Mrs Townend, who continued to live there with her husband's sister, sparing it from the fate of being knocked down.

But the 15 acres of adjoining land which had been used for the caravan park was sold separately by Burges Estates for development. When it closed in 1974 there were 375 caravans and a shop on the site. Many of the regular visitors were very sad to lose contact with the good friends they had made there over the years for the camp was highly regarded for its 'select' standards and friendly atmosphere.

North Shoebury Post Office
Palace Cinema and war memorial

Chapter 10
SHOEBURY EXPANDS

With Southend running out of development land to house the increasing population, eyes turned to Shoebury and the remaining empty spaces for building land. Extensive plans were drawn up to replace the remaining open fields of North Shoebury with housing developments.

The past thirty years have seen these fields and farmland slowly disappear, as the whole area, a section at a time, was stripped bare of the valuable layer of brickearth before being released for development, plot by plot. Now the whole area is built on apart from the open space of the old playing fields and the new sports ground, a mixture of private and public developments covering a wide price range.

The Painters Estate has spread west from Wakering Road meeting the Friars Estate, which in turn linked arms with the Eagle Estate. To the north of this more new roads and houses fringe the south of Poynter's Lane as far as the junction with Star Lane.

Controversy dogged the planned sale of houses on Bishopsteignton, a development built between Maplin Way and North Shoebury Road in the early 80s.

The old aspirations to the gentility of our western neighbours at Thorpe Bay appears to have persuaded Southend-on-Sea Estates to forget quite where they were and to move the town boundary over a little, the development being known as 'Thorpe Bay Garden Suburb'. Their 1982 advertising brochure for the estate read: 'Combining the atmosphere of an established country town with the amenities of an important commercial and social centre, Thorpe Bay can justifiably be considered a most desirable and exclusive residential area'.

The growth of North Shoebury with the opening of the large superstore there has resulted in a decline in business at the High Street, West Road and Ness Road shopping parades, with many of the smaller shops having closed.

In South Shoebury vacant land available for building was at a premium. When the old houses in Vincent Crescent were demolished, the allotments that for many years had been behind the south of the street were included in the rebuilding scheme that is now Vincent Close and Maya Close.

Further south in Ness Road, on the land left vacant by the Hall Farm Caravan Park when it closed after the lease ran out, the Admirals Housing Estate was built by a consortium of builders in March, 1974.

Chapter 11
THE CHURCHES OF SHOEBURY

Although the Garrison church has finally closed, Shoebury has ten active churches in the two parishes. Some have stayed on their original site but the buildings have been extended as the congregation has grown, others have moved location to serve the needs of the new estates north of Elm Road.

The ancient church of St Mary the Virgin, North Shoebury, probably the oldest building in Shoebury, is home to a thriving, modern congregation. Isolated as it was in open countryside, worshippers had once dwindled to only four. Now, with the church kept in good repair and a modern church hall replacing the corrugated iron parish room from Victorian times, it serves the new surrounding population as well as many from beyond the parish borders.

The present building of Kentish ragstone and flint rubble dressed with limestone is not thought to be the original church that stood on the site. Once under the protection of Thomas à Becket, Archbishop of Canterbury, it passed into the hands of Prittlewell Priory in the 12th century, after which it appears to have been rebuilt. First the chancel was built, then the nave was added, and in 1254 three archways were set into the south wall of the nave opening into a new south aisle. This extension was later demolished and the arcades blocked up again, but additions and refinements, including the tower, were made over the following years until the Reformation, when all the church plate appears to have been sold or stolen - a not an uncommon occurrence in churches as this time, since the break with the Church of Rome and the introduction of the new Protestant Common Prayer Book in 1548. According to records, St. Mary's appears to have been allowed to decline on several occasions over the years into a very poor state of repair. Under the auspices of the Benton family and the new Vicar, Henry Wilmott, extensive renovations were undertaken in 1884 and the old vicarage was pulled down, the new replacement having already been built. More recently maintenance to the walls, roof and the tower took place in 1982.

Inside, the church has an ancient square font of Purbeck marble. A fine marble slab dated 1746 forms the top of the communion table. Costing £50 this was given by John Ibbetson Esq., who is buried in the chancel. When he died in 1804, aged 68, his estates passed to his sister, Elizabeth Jones, whose husband, a captain in the Royal Artillery, had been killed at the Battle of Bunker Hill, in 1775.

St Andrew's Church, built in 1100, was also built of flint rubble and Kentish ragstone. It too has been enlarged and embellished over time. In the 13th century arched recesses were made in the east wall and both sides of the nave, the lancet window on the south side of chancel and the west tower were added in the 14th

St Mary the Virgin, North Shoebury

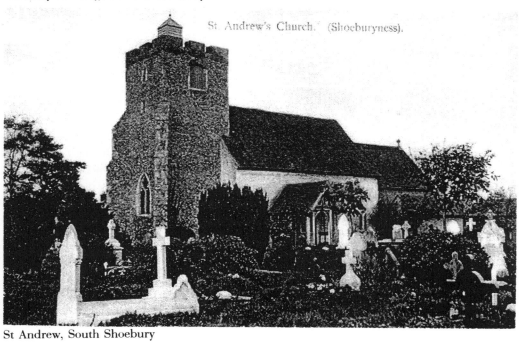

St Andrew, South Shoebury

century. Separated from the nave by a Norman arch the embattled tower has a brick parapet and blocks of chalk line the walls.

During the 15th century the church was re-roofed in oak and the timber porch added. The carving over the porch depicts a mesh net containing a fish, and on either side the shields feature fish and the cross of St Andrew, emphasising the church's association with the sea and St Andrew, the fisherman.

Until the dissolution of the monasteries the Priory held the church, sometimes reducing the status of the incumbent from a rector to a vicar, which then enabled it to collect tithes from the parish for the benefit of the monastery. Since the Reformation there have been more restorations, and many gifts have been made by parishioners and church organisations over the centuries to beautify the inside. Sadly, during the last major restoration many of the interesting contents were destroyed. The Victorian font is of Norman design with an oak cover.

Two of the three original church bells were blown down in 1749. The church register records the event: 'On 10th June, 1749, two of the bells in ye church had been blown down and crack'd. They were this day, by a faculty from the Bishop, sent to London to be sold and ye money to be laid out for beautifying ye church. The fees for the faculty £41.10s.8d.'

Until 1871 singing was accompanied by a barrel organ; the new replacement, a harmonium, was deemed too mournful by the congregation, so a new organ was bought in 1919, and renewed in 1933 at a cost of £130.

The main approach was originally from the shore road, beside the Hall. Two large black gates were at the entrance with a stone mounting block for those who travelled by horse or carriage, and where Shoebury Hospital now stands; rings were set into the wall to tether the horses. On the north side of the church three steps helped parishioners over the wall, from where a path led across the common to the Parsonage at the Grove, and beyond to Friars Farm. In the opposite direction a path led to Dangers Farm.

During building work in April, 1903, when the vestry was being added, the Reverend Galway Popham, M.A., received an anonymous letter which read: 'Sir, I saw in *The Globe* that the working men in your parish helped to build a vestry. They must be jolly good fellows and you must be the right sort to have influenced them. I send you £1. I would like you to surprise them and give them a poundsworth of tobacco'. A very generous donation at the day's prices.

When extensive roof repairs were carried out in 1965 the weathervane, depicting a fishing boat under sail, was erected in memory of Captain Townend from the adjacent Hall, who had died that year.

In 1862 the first church services were held in the new schoolroom on the present St Peter's Church site in Hinguar Street. The curate, Mr E C Wells, held morning and evening services and afternoon Sunday school, the expense of providing for this being borne mainly by Dale Knapping, assisted by an annual subscription from the Reverend E B Wynne of St Andrew's. The Curate's Aid Society made a yearly donation towards the salary of the curate. Two years later, when Mr Wells became the rector of North Shoebury, morning services were discontinued, while evening services were conducted by the Reverend Thackeray, the Vicar of Shopland.

In 1899 the services in the schoolroom were discontinued when a new church was erected in Dane Street, built by A J Harris, the church organist. Three years later it was pulled down and rebuilt again in the High Street, opposite the police station (previously the council chambers), where it continued to hold services until 1919. Then the original National School in Hinguar Street was converted to the present church building and dedicated for worship on 3rd December.

The High Street premises then served as the church hall until it was blown down in the hurricane of 1987. A portacabin was pressed into emergency service until a new hall was completed in the garden behind the church.

There are now flats on the site of the old church hall.

With no local church to administer to the Catholic troops and their families, the Garrison authorities arranged for a visiting priest, Father Last, to give Mass to them and some civilians in the gymnasium. This chaplain came to the Garrison from Chelmsford, staying overnight to rest at a farm at Bournes Green, the home of the Daines family. After taking the service he had a long ride on horseback to Chelmsford where he was also chaplain.

In 1862 the Garrison allocated funds for a local priest to look after the soldiers. In May that year Father Muir took his first Mass in an upstairs front room in his small house in Southend, converted for use as a chapel. After hearing confession and giving Holy Communion there to his Southend flock he would walk the four miles to the Garrison to say mass at 9 am. By 11.30 am, after walking the four miles back, he would be back at his small upstairs chapel to give another Mass. In time the Army afforded him the taxi fare back home.

Shoebury had its first Catholic Church dedicated to St George and the English Martyrs in 1891. Made of corrugated iron and wood, the building provided by the MoD stood on the site of the present church. It was enlarged in 1908 and a transept added as a sacristy, which sufficed until the current building was completed in 1939. Under Father Toft's energetic administration fund raising events had raised the badly needed money to assist with church finances. By 1928 he had also built the new presbytery and a chapel of ease, St Gregory's, in Thorpe Bay.

In 1910 a group of friends began to hold Baptist meetings to bring some comfort to one of them who fell sick. This was at 36 Wakering Avenue, the home of Mr Williams, the regimental photographer at the Experimental Establishment, and from these gatherings grew the first church of just seven people.

In December they began to meet in a billiard room known as 'The Old Boys Club' in West Road, and the following year they progressed to a meeting room at number 83 (the first Peculiar Peoples' Chapel) for the costly sum of 8/9d a week (less than 44p). This rose to 12/- (60p), a large amount for such a small congregation.

In 1927 a JP from Hutton, Mr H E Wood, made a gift of an acre of land to build a new church. It opened on 14th November, 1928, at a cost of £1,578 in Thorpedene Gardens, at that time in the middle of open fields

During the war with so many men away and families evacuated, only six women remained to 'hold the fort'. The church was used as a first aid post, and Caulfield Road School opposite was converted to a hospital ward to prevent the military taking it over. After the war the congregation returned and grew, and by 1950 it was necessary to add the Youth Hall, costing £2,850, opened by Mr Wood's daughter, Mrs Scroggie.

In 1954 the Manse was built to accommodate the first full-time minister. A Fellowship Hall was added in 1974 to provide extra facilities and meeting rooms, and eleven years later the new Sanctuary was built at a cost of £230,000. Since then a further new extension has been added to link the old and new buildings together. Now a new church is established on the Friars Estate as an offshoot of the main church after services were held in the Community Hall on Easter Sunday, 1987. By September, 1991, they were established as a separate congregation in their own right, serving the needs of people in the Elm Road area.

The Methodist movement has two followings, the Wesleyans and the Primitive Sect. The first meetings of the Wesleyan Methodists in Shoebury were held in a lecture hall in the garrison. From this meeting place they moved to a mission hall in the High Street until the opening of their first chapel there in 1892/3.

It cost £1,000 to build and could seat 250. A schoolroom was added in 1911. When it was closed for worship the congregation joined that of the Methodist Church in St Andrew's Road. For many years the old building was used as a storage facility for stage props belonging to the Rochford impresario, Jerry Jerome, before being demolished and the flats on the corner of Gunners Road built in its place.

The Primitive Sect was brought to Shoebury and Great Wakering as extensions of the Southend church started by the Reverend Thomas Jackson, who ran the Whitechapel Mission. He had purchased a house on the corner of Pleasant Road to use as a convalescent home for sick people from the East End who would benefit from a holiday in the bracing sea air. The Southend church, situated behind the house, is now the Grosvenor Rock factory. The first Shoebury services were held in a loft above a stable in St Andrew's Road. That stable, now converted to a garage, is still there opposite the present church that was built in 1899.

Before the Salvation Army began holding meetings in Shoebury in 1882 members had to walk 14 miles to attend the nearest Cottage Meetings. A band was formed that year with just four instruments; these were placed in a closed room and each man entered the room in turn to choose the instrument he fancied most, the last man found he had been left the bass. All but the bass player knew one hymn to get them through the first meeting but he, poor chap, could manage only the 'C' scale. Fortunately for him, with little time to practice for their first appearance, the tune to be rendered was in that scale. With no real musical knowledge, the growing band enlisted the help of an instructor from 'outside', the gentleman in the top hat. It is recorded that band practice was often interspersed with the players on bended knee praying for his conversion.

At this time the local branch was not recognised as a Corps. A golden sovereign found by one of the bandsmen was used the pay two fares to the Exeter Hall, in the Strand, where the Founder was conducting meetings and a request was made for an officer at Shoebury.

The band was invited to play at the opening of the Gravesend Corps. Whether it was as a result of their rendition it is not known, but one sister had her bonnet ripped from her head with a carving knife in the melée that ensued. Fireworks were thrown, along with any other available missile and the band eventually fled, leaving their instruments to be collected by cart the next day.

When Bandmaster Whent took over in 1902 the tune book that was passed on to him had this written inside, 'Let him that lacketh wisdom ask of God, who giveth liberally, and upbraideth not' (extract taken from *The Musician of The Salvation Army*, 22nd October, 1938).

After many years of meeting in Ness Road the Army has new premises in Frobisher Way. The current band has six musicians.

In 1849 John Banyard formed the Peculiar People in Rochford and a chapel was built in North Street that year, funded from the money of his second wife, Judith Knapping. The Knapping family also assisted in financing the Shoebury chapel at 83 West Road. This was demolished in the 1970s and today Sander's Store stands on the site.

In 1931 Bishop Heddle (who ran a draper's shop in Southend) offered three building plots in West Road for a new chapel and schoolroom to be built. The builder, Ernest Everitt, completed the work in only three months before accepting his payment of £600. There were two sects of this denomination formed in 1938, the Original and Liberty Sects. In 1956 the name was changed to the Union of Evangelical Churches.

The Shoebury Mission Hall had its beginnings in 1918 when a Westcliff family began holding Communion services on Sunday mornings in a house in John Street,

St Peter & St Paul, Shoeburyness Garrison, showing stove pipes and cowl that were removed in March, 1889

Chancel of Garrison Church, 1892

open to anyone who wished to attend. In the afternoon a Sunday school class was held in Alp's Hall in the High Street. Later in the day there was an evening service, also held there.

George Alp was the local undertaker and used the premises during the week to carry out his trade, a reminder of this greeted members each week as they climbed the wooden stairs inside the hall and passed by the coffins lined against the wall.

The move to the present church, Shoebury Hall, Wakering Avenue, is remembered every year with an Anniversary Conference held to commemorate the first services held there on the first Saturday in October, 1920. Membership grew to over 100 and included local tradesmen, the manager of Shoebury Waterworks, soldiers and railway workers, and the manageress of the 'Soldier's Home', a lodging house in the High Street.

The new church was very active in the community with three meetings a week for Bible teaching, readings and prayer, a women's meeting, special services for the railway workers (with tea provided), and open air witness in the High Street. A familiar sight on summer Sunday evenings was the small group, accompanied by their portable harmonium, holding a service in Rampart Terrace on the open space above the concrete steps leading down to the beach. The children had their own meeting on Wednesdays and on one occasion seven coaches were needed to take over 200 children to Maldon on the annual Sunday School outing.

There are no paid ministers, services are taken by any competent member for those who wish to join in worship and witness according to the principles laid down in the New Testament. No offerings are taken at services, the members considering it their responsibility to maintain the testimony.

Before the Garrison had a church of its own, the officers and men would attend services at St Andrew's, where some served as churchwardens. Church Parades were usually held in a gun shed on the Hilly Marsh testing range, and some services were held in the black huts barrack block. Originally the Church of St Peter and St Paul, finished in July, 1866, by the builders, Jackson and Shaw, was intended for use as a chapel school, but it was never used for that purpose. It was adopted instead as a church for the army, but it was a cold, bare place to worship in.

Mr E H F Jenner, the chaplain in 1883, added an altar cloth and dossal, a small brass cross and some brass vases, but it was still an uninviting place when, a year later, the new chaplain, the Reverend A Malim, was posted here on his return from Bermuda.

My great-grandfather, Harry, was his manservant/batman in Bermuda and accompanied him to Shoebury on his return to England. Harry then married my great-grandmother, Hannah, who kept a record of all the purchases, and the prices paid, as the Reverend Malim slowly transformed the church into a place he deemed worthy of worship; her diary helped to establish a record of the church.

He enthusiastically raised funds for the new furbishments and was very successful, but there was never enough for everything he hoped to achieve. So he sent a request to Bermuda asking for the release of the funds he had raised there for the proposed building of a new Garrison Church in St George's, in memory of the officers who had died of yellow fever. After he left there seemed little chance of this coming to fruition, so the funds were duly sent for the benefit of the Shoebury Church. The original £350.19.2d had grown to £493.16.7d with interest, which enabled work to start on the oak roof and windows.

The east window depicts the Nativity with the Adoration of the Shepherds and Magi, and the Ascension. The work cost £94.3.4d. In the smaller window of the north wall of the sanctuary he picked as the subject for one section St Alban, the patron saint both of the Royal Engineers and the Diocese of Chelmsford. For the other section he chose St Barbara, patron saint of the Royal Artillery, selecting a copy of the picture, painted by Palma Vecchio, who used his daughter Violante as the model, which hangs in the church of St Maria Formoso, Venice. The Gunners' colours depicting guns and cannons and a red zig-zag line are supposed to represent the thunder and lightning that roared and flashed as St Barbara was executed for her beliefs. The walls of the chancel were decoratively painted, and other paintings were hung on canvas depicting the four saints of Great Britain. Sadly, many of these disappeared when the Royal Engineers redecorated the church in 1924.

When the Reverend Malim was posted to Cairo in 1893 his work was continued by his successor, Mr W M Churchward. The Secretary of State directed that a plan should be kept of the Rev Malim's intended scheme for future windows, which was adhered to with the exception of the West window, installed in 1906, dedicated to the memory of those who fell in the South African War.

When the centenary chapel was dedicated in 1966 consideration was still given to the Rev Malim's intentions. The church is now closed, the last service held there was on Christmas Eve, 1997. The carefully assembled accoutrements are now packed away, maybe to grace another chapel one day, or to be sold.

Garrison Church choir, 1894

Chapter 12
TODAY AND WHAT THE FUTURE MAY HOLD

It is now many years since the last regiment served in the garrison (1975), although a limited presence remained until 1st April, 1998, when the gates of the Horseshoe Barracks and the Old Ranges closed for the last time and an air of abandonment hangs over the once thriving establishment as decision is awaited on the future use of the land.

After they formed a joint working party in September, 1996, the MoD and Southend Borough Council worked together to try and find a suitable and fitting rôle for the land and the listed buildings there, which are in the preservation area of Shoeburyness, the hope being that they would be retained and one day put to good use again, to provide once more a source of employment for the local population.

In July, 1998, the Ministry of Defence confirmed its intentions to go ahead with plans to sell 76 hectares of the land and a draft-planning brief was issued that September for public consultation and suggestion on possible uses. Hopes that a training unit in weapons testing, situated in Rochester, might move to the garrison site were dashed in August, 1998. However, hope still remained that the Defence Ordnance Disposal School might move instead to the former top secret Atomic Weapons Establishment on Foulness Island, closed down under a previous defence review.

As feared, more job losses were announced at the New Ranges, a further 186 jobs to go leaving a workforce of just 137 people to carry out the much reduced testing. There were fears that proposals put forward to privatise the Defence Evaluation and Research Agency would threaten even more jobs. Local opposition to the noise from the guns at the New Ranges is putting pressure on the government to move the ranges to another site.

Taking a ride out to Wakering Stairs today, past Landwick Cottages, one of the areas devastated by the 1953 floods, one passes the names of the old gun battery emplacements that now stand derelict. You cross over the now rusting rail lines that once carried the armaments and equipment from Barge Pier to their testing locations facing the mudflats. Still visible from the sea wall are the markers for the Broomway and the beginning of this old roadway. What future lies ahead for these watery wastelands now?

Light industry provides jobs in the factories in Campfield Road, and on the Towerfield and Vanguard Industrial Estates, but there is still much unemployment in the area with few job opportunities available locally. The town has a large percentage of young people, of which 14.5% of the 16-25 year age group were unemployed in 1998. A new Information Shop opened in West Road to assist job seekers, with outside agencies offering advice on careers as well as opportunities and activities for young people. A training roomwas provided for courses to be held there.

Now in receipt of a second grant of £800,000, from the Government's Single Regeneration Budget Challenge Fund, it is hoped to provide even more facilities. Two community and family centres, one each for North and South Shoebury for social and recreational activities, an upgrade for Shoebury park with a cafeteria and to generally improve economic growth locally to provide a brighter future for the town's population of 18,700.

Five schools serve the infant and junior needs of the town: Hinguar Street, Richmond Avenue, Thorpedene, Friars, and St George's Roman Catholic Infant School. Caulfield Road School has grown to become a large Comprehensive School with over 1,100 pupils, now bidding for technology college status.

For some years the old rifle range to the east of Ness Road has been leased to Southend Borough Council for use as the aptly named Gunners Park. All efforts to get the beach area contained within the Ministry of Defence boundary returned for public use were refused because of the risk of unexploded material still being present. It is hoped that one day, under new ownership, the park and access to the foreshore will be secured as a permanent public amenity.

Meanwhile, the Common still welcomes holidaymakers, mainly day visitors out along the promenade from Southend, and local people. There are still beach huts and a cafeteria, but the boating pool and putting green, features from the 30s, have disappeared. East Beach, so conveniently near the station, is very popular with a caravan park, a large grassy play area and cafeteria. This is still the driest, sunniest corner of England.

OUR OLD LANDMARKS FROM THE PAST

All but one of the old landmarks we have followed through the ages still remain today, only North Shoebury Hall is missing.

Mr Roy Millbank farms Tithe Farm in Poynter's Lane, and the land stretching round to Wick Farm in Wakering. Now his crops are wheat and rape, peas for the dried market and field beans used for animal feed. The latter are specific varieties grown and harvested when they become hard.

South Shoebury Hall is now a listed building, protected by the Department of the Environment. 'An 18th century red brick front to a mediæval timber framed house, probably 16th century'. It would be easy to miss this picturesque old building as you drive past; tucked back from the road it lies sandwiched between the former Sunshine Homes, now the Shoebury Hospital, and the houses in Church Road at the junction with Ness Road. It rests now in just an acre of garden, all that is left of a once extensive estate. All the Hall's former lands have been sold for development, Cambridge Town to the north, and the Admirals Estate to the south.

The current owners, the Dedman family, won an award in 1989 for their painstaking work in restoring the property. The old bakery with the red brick oven in one corner serves now as the entrance hall to the original, frame and weatherboarded section of the house. Still visible is the stone cobbled floor made from the ballast brought in by barges long ago. The old oak floors are bedded down on a mixture of earth reinforced with cockleshells, while the old dairy has still kept unchanged the floor of terracotta pammets.

In the sitting room is the large inglenook fireplace that many a farmer would have sat by in days gone by. In an upstairs bedroom a beam bears the scars of hot dripping wax from tapers and candles that once burned brightly in their sconces for illumination. On the roof clumps of houseleeks sprout from the tiles: rumour says that should these disappear the house will be taken by the devil.

The Moated House, built by Samuel Benton in 1824 and now known as Moat House, is opposite the Asda superstore on North Shoebury Road.

The White House, known as Barbours in mediæval times, is just to the west of the roundabout at Parson's Corner on Bournes Green Chase.

Opposite, shrouded by trees, is the Old Vicarage, now being sympathetically restored by the present owners. The old well and pond are still there in the garden.

To the east of Parson's Corner, in Poynter's Lane, is North Shoebury House. Once Philip Benton's home, this belonged in more recent years to the Hutley family, who also farmed North Shoebury Farm. For a while it passed out of their hands, only to be bought back again later by another family member who lived there for many years. When the family retired to Devon it passed into new ownership.

The Red Brick House, standing at the junction of the High Street and Elm Road, has changed little over the years apart from a new front wall made necessary when a lorry demolished the front fence.

The old manor house Suttons still stands within the New Ranges, quite easily visible through the wire fence by the boom, and from Wakering Road you can just catch a glimpse of the weathervane and chimney pots. It was requisitioned during the war for the use of army officers and, under later occupants, damage occurred and the magnificent staircase and panelling were removed.

The pond and bridge at Well House (opposite the entrance to Linton Road in Ness Road) are now obscured from sight by overgrown trees and shrubs.

Crouchman's, since the 50s known as 'The Lansdowne', now caters for a different clientele since it became a nursery school. Next door there is still a small caravan park.

The Picture Palace still stands at the junction of Campfield Road and Ness Road, no longer peddling celluloid 'dreams' but canvas 'palaces' and chemical loos for those who dream of green pastures further afield. Today it is still clearly recognisable, the outside appearance has changed little, but inside the auditorium has been converted into two storeys, a false floor having been inserted. Only a few reminders of its former glory remained intact after conversion, the only clues to its past being the sloped floor for the balcony seating left at the top of the original stairs, and the projection box. Currently the building is in use as a camping showroom and shop.

Opposite, the *Duke of Cambridge* has had his day, the hotel, more recently known as the *Shoe and Cobbler* is no more. On the site is a rest home for the elderly.

The former Sunshine Convalescent Home was renamed the Shoebury Hospital in 1948, since 1959 it has provided care for the elderly. Now known as Shoebury House under Southend Health Authority, the ground floor serves as a day centre for the elderly, therapies and treatment are available and a chiropodist visits weekly. The first floor comes under the Mental Health Community Services with community psychiatric nurses based there, an outpatients clinic operates with a weekly visit from a psychiatrist.

The Military Families Hospital in Campfield Road is now *The Captain Mannering*. The red cross painted on the roof to indicate its previous calling is still just visible.

Rebuilt after being pulled down in 1946 *Shore House* is now a bright, modern pub and restaurant overlooking Shoebury Common.

The old weatherboarded post office, shop and blacksmith's forge that was Shoebury Cross House at Parson's Corner is now restored and in use as *The Angel* public house. A full picture history of the renovation work can be seen inside on the walls of the dining area.

Christopher Parson's Barn on North Shoebury Hall Farm, rebuilt in 1763, now stores different varieties of grain products. As the fields surrounding it were gradually sold for housing it fell into disrepair until it was purchased and restored by Clifton Inns and reopened as a public house on 6th December, 1983. Mr Parsons, who died in 1787 aged 88, is buried in the nearby chancel of St Mary's Church, close by lie his ancestors and descendants.

The two Norman churches still stand, the surrounding flocks larger now, but other denominations have joined to help minister to their needs.

***

So we have seen our two small hamlets, Great and Little Shoebury, merge and grow over nearly two thousand years.

In the year 2000 the garrison site has been sold to a developer and his proposed plans are on the drawing board. Will they provide Shoebury with the new identity it needs for the new Millennium? The battle now is between local residents and the new owner to find acceptable uses for the site.

What will the future bring, I wonder? It will fall to someone else to tell that story.

Maureen Orford,
2000

Because my grandfather's intended book was not completed he had not made a list of the written sources he used, or the donors of the photographs he had been given for inclusion. Some I have discovered through my own reading and I have acknowledged those, I apologise for any unintentional omissions where I do not know the origin of the material.

Benton, Philip, The History of the Rochford Hundred, 1867, updated by Rochford Historical Society, South, 1978, North, 1981
Burrows, J W, Southend-on-Sea & District, 1909
Clack, Edward, Spy in the sky, 1992
Coller, D W, The People's history of Essex, 1861
Dilley, Roy, The Dream Palaces of Southend, undated
Emmison, F G, Elizabethan life in Essex, 1970
Emmison, F G, Home, work and land, Hart, 1976
Emmison, F G, Morals and church courts, 1973
Glennie, Donald, Our Town, 1947
Grieve, Hilda, The Great Tide, 1959
Herbert, A P, War story of Southend Pier, 1945
Morris, Rev. David, A history of England, 1886
Oman, Charles, A history of England. 19th ed., 1895
Peile, Major A J, The School of Gunnery Shoeburyness, 1913
Phillips, C., Recollections of the village area, 1996, Shoebury Society
Pollitt, W, Southchurch and its past, 1949
Stenton, Sir Frank, Anglo-Saxon England, 1971
Turner, F *and* Stewart,W, The Maunsell forts, 1996
Victoria County History of Essex, 1903,7 & 63 Vols. 1-3
Wright, Thomas, The County of Essex, 1836
Anon. Early recollections of the School of Gunnery, 1903
A summary of the archæological dig at the garrison conducted by Gifford & Partners, sponsored by the MoD

Unloading a barge by sheers, 1880

ACKNOWLEDGEMENTS

I would like to thank everyone who has helped me to complete this book. Those who answered my many questions, either in person or by phone, many of whom I never met. To the people who sent me information about the churches in the town. The people of Shoebury who shared their memories, Ann Allen, Peter Allen, Grace Coppock, Elizabeth Wilding and Hilda Cripps. Also those who sent me pictures, in particular to Mr Partridge, who lent me his postcard collection for many months having never met me before, to Mrs Stibbards, who lent me a selection of photographs and Mr E Clack for his aerial photographs.

To the staff at Essex Records Office, the Technical Services Department at Southend Borough Council and the *Southend Standard* group of newspapers for giving me permission to use material.

To Tony Hill for checking the facts about the Garrison, and the use of photos.

To Mr and Mrs Dedman who showed me around their home at South Shoebury Hall.

To friends who assisted me with computer work, Peter Hall and Peter McBane. And to my husband who chauffeured me around, listened often, and magically restored the programme each time I hit the wrong button on the computer and yet again appeared to have lost everything I had written over the months.

H A Blencowe with his collection of army badges